Pattern-Free

EDITED BY **JEANNE STAUFFER**

Sewing™

HOUSE of
WHITE
BIRCHES

PUBLISHERS
SINCE 1947

PATTERN-FREE SEWING

Copyright © 2005 House of White Birches, Berne, Indiana 46711

EDITOR	Jeanne Stauffer
MANAGING EDITOR	Barb Sprunger
TECHNICAL EDITORS	Barbara Weiland, Mary Travis
COPY EDITORS	Conor Allen, Michelle Beck, Nicki Lehman
PHOTOGRAPHY	Tammy Christian, Carl Clark, Christena Green, Matt Owen
PHOTO STYLISTS	Terri Huey, Tammy Nussbaum
ART DIRECTOR	Brad Show
ASSISTANT ART DIRECTOR	Karen Allen
PUBLISHING SERVICES MANAGER	Brenda Gallmeyer
GRAPHIC ARTS SUPERVISOR	Ronda Bechinski
GRAPHIC ARTIST	Debby Keel
PRODUCTION ASSISTANTS	Marla Freeman, Cheryl Kempf, Marj Morgan
TECHNICAL ARTISTS	Chad Summers, Liz Morgan
CHIEF EXECUTIVE OFFICER	John Robinson
PUBLISHING DIRECTOR	David J. McKee
BOOK MARKETING DIRECTOR	Craig Scott
EDITORIAL DIRECTOR	Vivian Rothe
PUBLISHING SERVICES DIRECTOR	Brenda R. Wendling

Printed in the United States of America
First Printing: 2005
Library of Congress Number: 2004105974
ISBN: 1-59217-051-X

Welcome

Sometimes I get a craving to sew and I want to sew something right now. I don't want to look for a pattern or custom-fit the pattern to my measurements. I don't want to check the patterns I have to see if I can use one of them, and I really don't want to take the time to go to the store and buy a pattern. I want to sew, and I want to sew right now.

This desire to sit at my sewing machine and sew to my heart's content formed the basis for this book. Sewers are very creative; we don't always need or want a pattern when we sew something. We are passionate about sewing, not sewing because we need something to wear or something to give away, but sewing because we love to sew. The more hours we spend sewing, the happier we are!

With that in mind, I selected the projects for this book. Here is an entire book of projects that you can make without buying a pattern or using one you already have. Of course, you have to cut and measure before you sew. But this book is full of fun-to-make wearables and home dec projects that do not require a pattern. If you have thread and fabric in your stash that works, you can sit down and sew one of the projects from this collection right now.

So what are you waiting for? It's time to sew!

Warm regards,

Jeanne Stauffer

Contents

Crazy Block Chenille Throw

You don't need to knit or crochet to make this colorful, afghanlike throw. Four different flannel fabrics are layered, stitched and cut to make the raw edges of each block "bloom" into a colorful textured surface.

DESIGN BY JULIE WEAVER

PROJECT SPECIFICATIONS
Skill Level: Confident beginner
Throw Size: 54 x 60 inches

MATERIALS
Note: *All yardage is for 44/45-inch-wide fabric. Sew all seams together as directed below, using ½-inch-wide seam allowances.*

- 3½ yards each of 4 different woven flannel plaids or checks
- 7 yards of bias binding (see Step 10)
- All-purpose thread to match fabrics
- Walking foot with quilting guide (optional)
- Rotary cutter, mat and ruler
- Water-soluble marking pen
- Basic sewing supplies

INSTRUCTIONS
Project Note: *The throw is made of stacked squares and rectangles that are stitched and slashed and then sewn together to create larger sections. Each part of a section is made with stacks of the same four fabrics, but the color order in each stack is different in order to create the color variations for each section. Your fabric selection will determine the final*

look—and it may be surprising! That's the fun of making chenille fabric this way.

Step 1. Referring to Fig. 1 but disregarding the colors in the illustrations, cut one of each square or rectangle from each of the four plaid fabrics and position it in its section. Cut every piece from one fabric; repeat with each of the remaining three fabrics. When the cutting is finished, every stack should have pieces in the same order.

Step 2. For each block in the section, stack the four pieces with the color shown on the bottom of the stack. If you cannot "name" each of your fabrics a particular color, number them instead and plan your number rotation for each section. Stack each block in a section with the same color on the bottom and mix up the color rotation of the remaining three pieces in each stack as desired. If you stack them all the same within a section, the section will be one large "block" of the same color. Pin the layers together for each block.

Step 3. Using a water-soluble marking pen and a rotary ruler, draw a diagonal line in the center of each top square or rectangle as shown in Fig. 2. Attach the walking foot, if available, and stitch on the line through all layers on each set of squares or rectangle.

Step 4. Insert a quilting guide into the hole in the back of the presser foot or walking foot and adjust the guide so it sits ½ inch to the right of the needle. With the guide riding on the first row of stitching on one of the stacks, do a second row of stitching. Continue in this fashion until the stack is covered with rows of stitching spaced ½ inch apart. Repeat with each remaining stack.

Step 5. Using a sharp scissors and cutting only the top three layers of fabric in each stack, cut through the channels formed between the rows of stitching as shown in Fig. 4. Beginning at an outer edge, carefully insert the point of the scissors under the top three layers. Take your time to avoid catching the bottom layer.

Step 6. Paying careful attention to the direction of the diagonal rows, arrange the pieces for each section of the throw as shown in Fig. 1. Treating the uncut side of the pieces as the "right side" and using ½-inch-wide seams, sew the pieces together as shown for each section so the seam raw edges

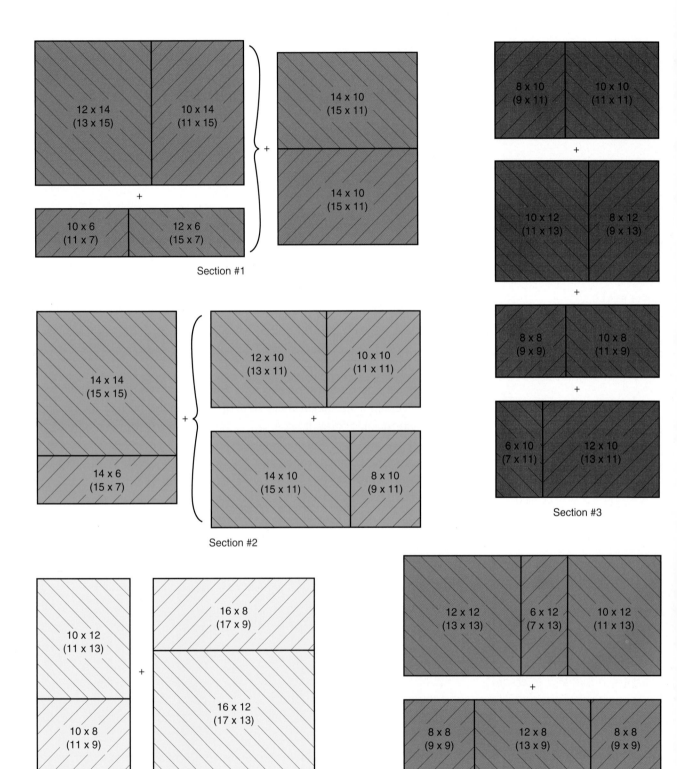

Fig. 1

are on the same side as the cut channels of the blocks.

Step 7. Using ½-inch-wide seams, sew Sections 1 and 2 together. Sew Section 3 to Section 1/2. Sew Sections 4 and 5 together. Sew Section 4/5 to Section 1/2/3. Staystitch ½ inch from the outer edge of the completed throw.

Step 8. Clip all seams to the stitching line, spacing the clips ¼ inch apart. **Note:** *Do not clip the outer edges.*

Step 9. Wash the completed throw in warm water on the normal cycle and dry at medium heat. **Note:** *Stop the dryer periodically during the cycle to clean the dryer lint trap. Remove all loose threads from the washer and dryer tubs before using them for the next load of clothes.*

Step 10. When the throw is completely dry, trim the outer edges as needed for a clean edge. Finish the edges with binding made from the fabric leftovers or make 7 yards of binding from a single fabric. ■

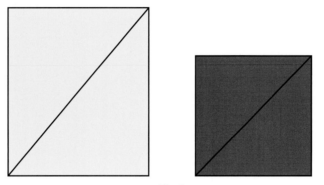

Fig. 2
Draw a diagonal line
through the center of the top
piece in each stack of squares or rectangles.

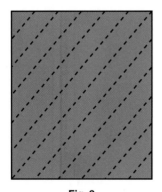

Fig. 3
Stitch through all layers in each stack,
spacing rows ¹/₂" apart.

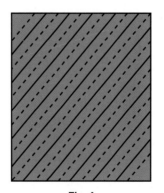

Fig. 4
Cut through the top three layers
only, cutting through the
center of each stitch-
outlined channel.

Rainbow Sailboats Ensemble

A regatta of colorful boats sails across a sea of blue in this easy-to-fuse-and-stitch appliquéd quilt. The quilt and matching valance are the perfect complements to a child's room.

DESIGNS BY JUDITH SANDSTROM

PROJECT SPECIFICATIONS

Skill Level: Confident beginner
Quilt Size: 60 x 75 inches
Valance Size: 18 x 48 inches

MATERIALS

QUILT

Note: *All yardage is for 44/45-inch-wide, tone-on-tone printed cotton fabric. Prewash all fabrics.*

- ¾ yard red for boats, sashing and borders
- ½ yard each of 5 colors (blue, yellow, green, orange, purple) for boats, sashing and borders
- 1½ yards light blue for block background
- ¾ yard white for sails
- ¼ yard black for boat masts
- 3¾ yards backing fabric
- 1¾ yards paper-backed fusible web
- 65 x 88-inch piece cotton batting
- All-purpose thread to match fabrics
- Clear nylon or polyester monofilament thread for quilting (optional)
- Rotary cutter, mat and ruler
- Basic sewing supplies

INSTRUCTIONS

Quilt

Project Note: *Cut all strips across the fabric width (40–44 inches depending on shrinkage.) Use ¼-inch-wide seam allowances and sew all seams with right sides together.*

Step 1. From the red fabric, cut one strip 6½ inches wide. From the strip, cut four 6½-inch squares for the border corners. From the remaining red and each of the five ½-yard cuts of fabric, cut four strips each 3½ inches wide. From two of the strips of each color, cut six 3½ x 12½-inch sashing strips. You should have two full-length strips of each color remaining for the pieced borders plus an additional piece of each fabric at least 4 inches wide for the boat bottoms. From the remaining yellow fabric, cut two 3½ x 6½-inch rectangles. Set aside with the border strips. Save the remaining yellow, plus all other remaining fabric, for Step 5.

Step 2. From the light blue fabric, cut four 12½-inch-wide strips. From each strip, cut three 12½-inch squares for a total of 12 squares.

Step 3. From the white fabric, cut two 3½-inch-wide strips. Cut 20 (3½-inch) squares for the sashing cornerstones from the strips. Cut one strip 9 inches wide and one strip 8 inches wide.

Step 4. From the fusible web, cut the following pieces: six 4 x 17-inch rectangles, two 9 x 17-inch rectangles, one 8 x 17-inch rectangle and one 7 x 9-inch rectangle.

Step 5. Following manufacturer's directions, apply paper-backed fusible web to the wrong side of each piece of the remaining fabric from Step 1. Trim each piece to 3½ x 17 inches. Referring to Fig. 1, cut two boat bottoms from each fusible-backed rectangle. Remove the paper backing from each piece.

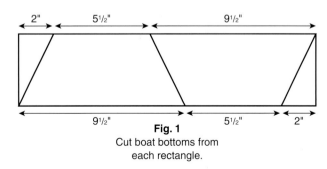

Fig. 1
Cut boat bottoms from each rectangle.

Step 6. Apply fusible web to the wrong side of the 9-inch-wide strip of white fabric. From the strip, cut six 5½ x 8½-inch rectangles. With the rectangles right side up, cut each rectangle in half diagonally as shown in Fig. 2. Remove the paper backing.

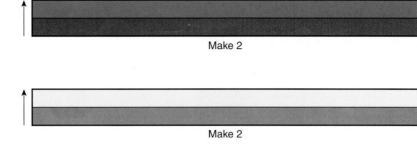

Make 2

Make 2

Make 2

Press in direction of arrows.

Fig. 4
Assemble the border strip units.

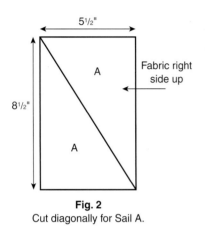

Fig. 2
Cut diagonally for Sail A.

Step 7. In the same manner as described in Step 6, apply fusible web to the wrong side of the 8-inch-wide strip of white fabric. Cut six 2¾ x 7½-inch rectangles. With the right side of the fabric facing up, cut diagonally as shown in Fig. 3. Remove the paper backing.

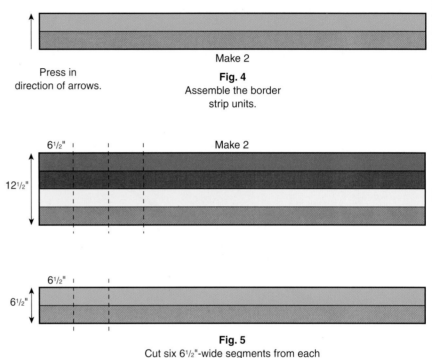

Make 2

Fig. 5
Cut six 6½"-wide segments from each strip unit.

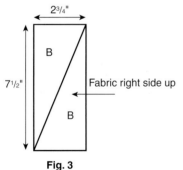

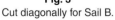

Fig. 3
Cut diagonally for Sail B.

Step 8. Apply fusible web to the wrong side of the black fabric and cut twelve ½ x 8½-inch strips

for the masts. Remove the paper backing.

Step 9. With right sides together, sew the remaining colored strips together in pairs as shown in Fig. 4. Press the seams in one direction.

Step 10. Sew each blue/red strip unit to a yellow/purple strip unit to make a unit that measures 12½ inches wide. Press the seams in one direction. From the resulting strip units, cut a total of twelve 6½ x 12½-inch segments for the pieced border as shown in Fig. 5. From the green/orange strip units,

cut a total of twelve 6½ x 6½-inch-segments for the pieced border.

Step 11. For each sailboat block, position a boat bottom, Sails A and B and a mast on a light blue square as shown in Fig. 6. **Note**: *All pieces should just touch each other without overlapping.* Fuse in place following the manufacturer's directions. Adjust the machine for a short, narrow zigzag stitch and zigzag around the outer edge of each piece. Use thread to match each color. Pull the thread tails to the wrong side and tie off securely.

Step 12. Referring to Fig. 7 for color placement, arrange the completed blocks in rows with the sashing strips and white corner-stones. Sew the pieces together in rows and press all seams toward the sashing strips. Sew the rows together to complete the quilt-top center.

Step 13. Again referring to Fig. 7 for color placement, arrange the strip-pieced units, the four yellow rectangles and the large red corner squares around the quilt top.

Sew the units together for the top and bottom edges of the quilt and sew a red square to each end. Press the seams in one direction and toward the corner squares at each end. Sew the remaining units together to make the side borders. Sew the side borders to the quilt and press the seams toward the sashing strips. Add

the top and bottom borders in the same manner.

Step 14. To prepare the backing, cut the backing fabric into two equal lengths and sew together at one set of selvages. Press the seam in one direction. The seam will lie across the width of the completed quilt.

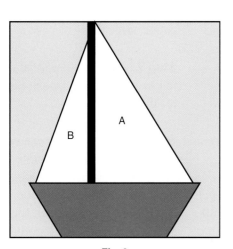

Fig. 6
Fuse sailboat pieces to
each light blue background square.

Fig. 7
Quilt Diagram

Step 15. Place the batting on a large, flat surface and smooth out any wrinkles. Place the completed quilt top right side up on top of the batting and baste the layers together ¼ inch from the quilt-top raw edges. Trim away the excess batting. Set aside temporarily.

Step 16. Smooth out the backing fabric on a large, flat surface with the right side up. Center the quilt top with batting, face down, on the right side of the batting. Smooth out any wrinkles and pin all layers together around the outer edge. Stitch, leaving a 15-inch-long opening in one edge for turning. Trim the excess backing fabric even with the quilt-top edges. Turn the quilt right side out through the opening and press the edges, turning in the raw edges. Slipstitch the opening edges together.

Step 17. Hand-baste vertically and horizontally through the center of each sashing rectangle to hold the layers together for machine quilting. Stitch in the ditch of all sashing and cornerstone seams. If you wish, you can also stitch in the ditch of the seams of some or all of the border rectangles for added emphasis. If desired, use clear nylon or polyester monofilament thread to avoid changing thread colors to match.

MATERIALS

VALANCE
Project Note: *All yardage is for 44/45-inch-wide, tone-on-tone printed cotton fabric. Prewash all fabrics. Sew all seams with right*

sides together using ¼-inch-wide seam allowances.

- ⅛ yard each of 6 colors (red, yellow, blue, green, orange and purple) for the boats and sashing
- ⅜ yard light blue for blocks
- ⅜ yard white for sails
- ⅛ yard black for boat masts
- ⅝ yard paper-backed fusible web
- 22-inch piece of ¼-inch-wide paper-backed fusible web
- 1¼ yards backing fabric (or ⅝ yard 54–60-inch-wide fabric)
- All-purpose thread to match fabrics
- Clear nylon or polyester monofilament thread for quilting (optional)
- Rotary cutter, mat and ruler
- Basic sewing supplies

INSTRUCTIONS
Valance
Note: *Cut all strips across the fabric width (40–44 inches depending on shrinkage.) Use ¼-inch-wide seam allowances and sew all seams with right sides together.*

Step 1. Cut two 3½ x 12½-inch rectangles from the red fabric. Repeat with the blue, orange and purple fabrics. From the green fabric and from the yellow fabric, cut one 3½ x 12½-inch rectangle. Set the remaining red, blue and green fabric aside for Step 5.

Step 2. From the white fabric, cut one strip 3½ inches wide. Cut eight 3½-inch squares from the strip.

Step 3. From the fusible web, cut one 9 x 17-inch strip, three 4 x 10-inch strips and one 2 x 9-inch strip.

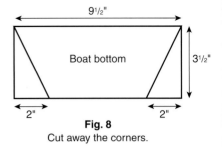

Fig. 8
Cut away the corners.

Step 4. Apply a 4 x 10-inch piece of fusible web to the wrong side of the remaining red, blue and green fabrics. Referring to Fig. 8, cut away the corners of each rectangle. Remove the backing paper.

Step 5. Following the manufacturer's directions, apply the 9 x 17-inch piece of fusible web to the wrong side of the remaining white fabric from Step 2. From this piece, cut two 5½ x 8½-inch and two 2¾ x 7½-inch rectangles. Cut each rectangle in half diagonally as shown in Fig. 2 for the quilt to make the triangles for the sails. Remove the backing paper from each piece.

Step 6. Apply fusible web to the wrong side of the black fabric and cut eight ½ x 8½-inch strips for the masts. Remove the paper backing.

Step 7. Make three sailboat blocks following the directions in Step 11 for the quilt.

Step 8. Arrange the blocks with sashing strips and cornerstones as shown in Fig. 9. Sew the pieces together in rows and press all seams toward the sashing strips. Sew the rows together to complete the valance panel.

Step 9. From the lining fabric, cut two strips each 18½ x 24½ inches. Sew the strips together along a set of short ends and press the seam to one side. (If your fabric is 55–60 inches wide, cut one strip 18½ x 48½ inches.)

Step 10. Pin the valance to the lining with right sides together and stitch as shown in Fig. 10, leaving 3-inch-long openings at the side edges for the curtain rod and a 10-inch-long opening in one long edge for turning.

Step 11. Apply a ¼ x 3-inch strip of fusible web next to the raw edge on the wrong side of the unstitched sections of the short openings on the lining and the valance as shown in Fig. 11. Before removing the backing

paper, make sure the strips are securely adhered to the fabric.

Step 12. Turn the valance right side out through the opening, turning under the raw edges at all opening edges. Press to fuse the turn-under allowance in place at each open edge at the sides

of the valance. Turn under, press and slipstitch the long opening edges together.

Step 13. Stitch in the ditch of the sashing seam at the upper edge of the valance as shown in Fig. 12 to create a casing for the curtain rod. ■

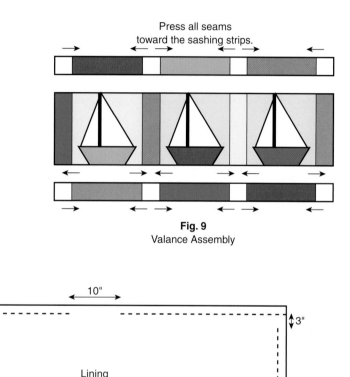

Fig. 9
Valance Assembly

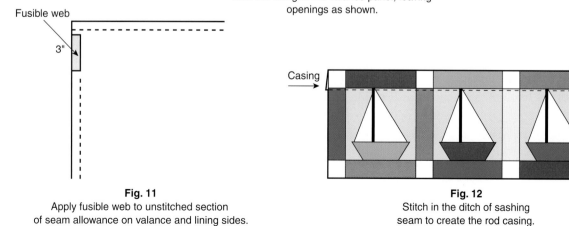

Fig. 10
Sew the lining to the valance panel, leaving openings as shown.

Fig. 11
Apply fusible web to unstitched section of seam allowance on valance and lining sides.

Fig. 12
Stitch in the ditch of sashing seam to create the rod casing.

Pleasant Dreams

Custom-made trim turns these simple pillowcases into decorative delights—too pretty to hide. Prairie points and a contrast band add to sweet dreaming.

DESIGN BY JULIE WEAVER

PROJECT SPECIFICATIONS
Skill Level: Beginner
Pillowcase Size: 21 x 31 inches

MATERIALS
Note: *Materials listed are for 44/45-inch-wide cotton fabric.*

- 2⅛ yards floral stripe
- ⅛ yard check or plaid for contrast band
- ⅝ yard total of contrasting print scraps for the prairie points
- All-purpose thread to match fabrics
- Optional: ¼-inch-wide precut strips of paper-backed fusible web
- Basic sewing supplies and tools

INSTRUCTIONS
Step 1. Prewash the fabric. Press to remove wrinkles.

Step 2. From the floral stripe, cut two 25½ x 43-inch strips and two 11 x 43-inch strips.

Step 3. From the contrasting check or plaid, cut two 2 x 43-inch strips.

Step 4. From the contrasting prints for the prairie points, cut a total of 28 (4½-inch) squares (14 for each pillowcase).

Step 5. With wrong sides together, fold each square in half diagonally and press. Fold in half again so all raw edges are even and press as shown in Fig. 1.

Step 6. On the right side of each 11 x 43-inch strip of floral stripe, arrange 14 prairie points as shown in Fig. 2. Each prairie point nests inside its neighboring point. The overlap in the prairie points is approximately 1½ inches but can be adjusted as needed so points fit along the edge and stop ½ inch from the short edges of the strip. Pin and machine-baste in place.

Step 7. With right sides together, pin one long edge of each 2-inch-wide contrast band to the lower band over the prairie points. Stitch

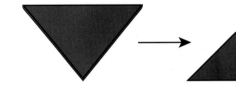

Fold square in half diagonally.   Fold in half again. Press.

Fig. 1
Fold squares to make prairie points.

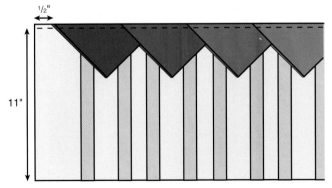

Fig. 2
Baste overlapping prairie points to lower pillowcase band.

¼ inch from the raw edges. Press the seam toward the band. With right sides together, sew a pillowcase panel to the upper edge of each band. Press the seam toward the band as shown in Fig. 3.

Step 8. Finish the lower edge of the lower striped band with serging or zigzagging.

Step 9. With right sides together and raw edges aligned, fold each pillowcase in half lengthwise and pin. Stitch ½ inch from the raw edges and finish the seam edges with serging or zigzagging.

Step 10. Turn the lower edge of each pillowcase to the inside with the finished edge just past the upper row of stitches. Press. Pin in place or use narrow strips of fusible web to fuse it in place.

Step 11. On the right side of the pillowcase, edgestitch along each edge of the contrast band, catching the pillowcase hem in place on the inside as shown in Fig.4. ■

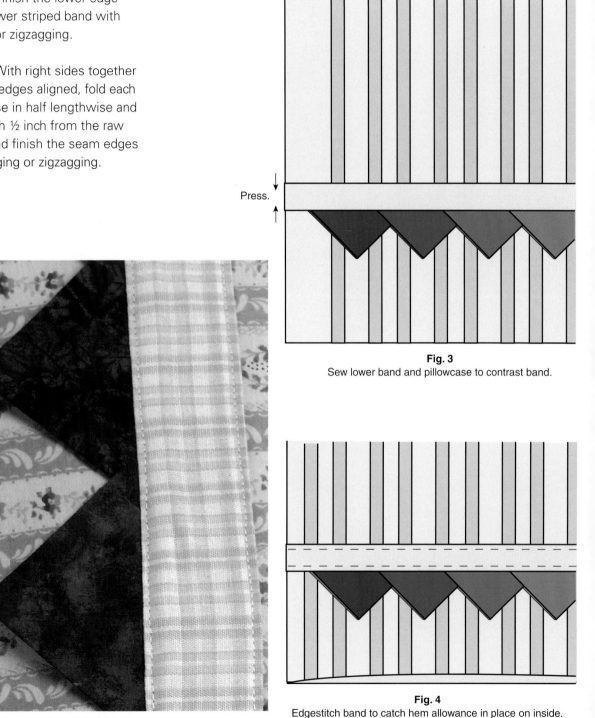

Press.

Fig. 3
Sew lower band and pillowcase to contrast band.

Fig. 4
Edgestitch band to catch hem allowance in place on inside.

Pacific Isle Bedroom Ensemble

Choose a trio of soft-colored island prints for this duvet cover, dust ruffle and pillow shams. You'll need a few measurements to customize the pieces to your bed size. Soon your room will be an oasis for refreshing nights caressed by tropical breezes.

DESIGNS BY CAROL ZENTGRAF

PROJECT SPECIFICATIONS
Skill Level: Intermediate
Duvet Cover, Pleated Dust Ruffle and Pillow Sham Sizes: Customized to your bed and pillow sizes.

MATERIALS

DUVET COVER
Note: *All yardage is for 54-inch-wide decorator fabric.*

Yardage listed below does not allow for print matching*. To allow for print matching at the piecing seams, measure the print design repeat and add this length to the yardage given below. For example, if the print repeat is 27 inches, add ¾ yard to the yardage for your bed size. Yardage is based on standard comforter sizes given in the chart on page 27 .*

- Print #1 for duvet cover front: 5½ yards for twin- or double-size bed; 6 yards for queen; 6¼ yards for king
- Print #2 for duvet cover back; 5½ yards for twin- or double-size bed; 6 yards for queen; 6¼ yards for king

- Coordinating solid for welting: 1¼ yards for twin or double; 1¾ yards for queen or king
- Jumbo welting: 7⅜ yards for twin; 7¾ yards for double; 8⅛ yards for queen; 8¾ yards for king
- ½-inch-wide paper-backed fusible web
- 1 yard self-adhesive hook-and-loop tape
- All-purpose sewing thread to match fabrics
- Zipper foot for your machine
- Basic sewing supplies and tools

INSTRUCTIONS
Duvet Cover
Project Note: *Use ½-inch-wide seam allowances throughout. Sew all seams with right sides together.*

Step 1. Referring to the Duvet Cover Cut Sizes Chart, use the *length* measurement for the cover size you are making and cut one full-width panel of fabric from Print #1 and from Print #2. For example, for a twin-size cover, you would cut the panels 95 inches long. The resulting panels will be 54 inches wide, plus the widths of the two unprinted selvage allowances on standard decorator fabric.

Step 2. For all sizes, cut an additional full-width panel of each fabric, making sure to cut it long enough to match the print of the first panel at each selvage edge if necessary. Cut the panel in half lengthwise. Turn under and press the selvage edge on each split panel.

Step 3. Apply fusible web to the turned-and-pressed edges of each split panel. Remove the paper backing and match the turned edge to the print in the full-width panel as shown in Fig. 1 on page 21. Fuse in place to hold the edges together for permanent stitching.

Step 4. On the wrong side, stitch the panels together along the fold line. Trim away the excess selvage edges, leaving a ½-inch-wide seam allowance. Press the seam allowances toward the split-width

panels. If necessary, trim the upper and lower edges of the split panels even with the center panel.

Step 5. Trim the completed duvet panel front and back panels to the cut width for your bed size as given in the duvet chart on page 27. Make sure to trim so the two split panels are the same width and the center panel is truly centered in the finished panel.

Step 6. At the upper edge of each panel, serge- or zigzag-finish the raw edge. Turn under and press

4 inches and topstitch in place. Sew the hook half of the hook-and-loop tape to the upper edge of the front panel and the loop half to the upper edge of the back panel. Position the upper edge of the tape strips ½ inch below the upper finished edge and take care to center each piece in its panel as shown in Fig. 2.

Step 7. Use a tape measure to determine the welting diameter and add 1 inch for seam allowances. Using this measurement, cut true bias strips from the contrasting

solid fabric. Referring to Fig. 3, cut and join strips with bias seams to make enough welting for the side and bottom edges of the duvet cover (side measurement x 2 inches + bottom-edge measurement + 3 inches).

Step 8. Wrap the bias strip around the welting with raw edges even and stitch the fabric layers together close to the welting, using a zipper foot as shown in Fig. 4.

Step 9. With raw edges even, pin the welting to the right side of the

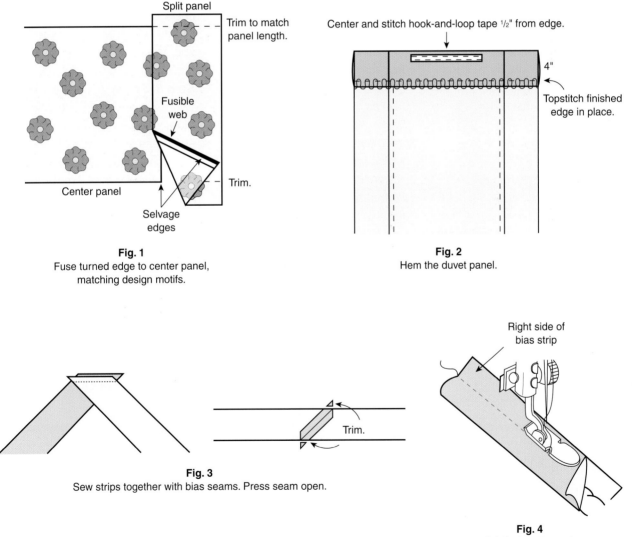

Fig. 1
Fuse turned edge to center panel, matching design motifs.

Fig. 2
Hem the duvet panel.

Fig. 3
Sew strips together with bias seams. Press seam open.

Fig. 4
Stitch close to cord.

duvet cover panel along the side and bottom edges. Round the bottom corners, clipping the welting seam allowance as needed. Angle the cut ends at the finished upper edges of the top as shown in Fig. 5. Using the zipper foot and a contrasting color thread in the bobbin, machine-baste in place.

Step 10. With right sides together, pin the duvet cover back to the duvet cover front. With the wrong side of the duvet cover front facing you so you can see the welting basting, stitch the layers together. Stitch just a thread or two past the basting, closer to the welting as shown in Fig. 6.

Step 11. Turn the cover right side out and remove any basting that shows. Press as needed and tuck your comforter inside.

MATERIALS

PLEATED DUST RUFFLE
Note: *All yardage is for 54-inch-wide decorator fabric and a dust ruffle with a finished skirt length* of 14 inches and the pleats shown in the instructions below. If your printed fabric requires matching the motifs at the seams, you will need to allow for extra yardage. If your bed requires a longer skirt, you will need to adjust the yardage requirement accordingly.

- 2¾ yards Print #3 for the dust ruffle skirt for twin or double bed sizes; 3⅛ yards for queen or king bed sizes
- Flat sheet in size to fit top of box springs for dust-ruffle deck
- Basic sewing supplies and tools

INSTRUCTIONS
Pleated Dust Ruffle
Project Note: *The featured dust ruffle skirt has a 14-inch finished drop from the edge of the box springs. Adjust the length of the drop as needed for your bed size. The end panel has an 8-inch-deep box pleat at the center. The side panels have two 8-inch-deep box pleats, a 1-inch-deep knife-edge pleat at the foot end and a 4-inch-deep knife-edge pleat at the head* end. The side and end panels overlap 2 inches at the corners.

Use ½-inch-wide seam allowances throughout. Sew all seams with right sides together.

Step 1. *For the twin or double bed sizes*, cut six strips, each 15 inches wide, across the fabric width. *For the queen or king bed sizes*, cut seven strips.

Step 2. Sew the strips together as required and trim as needed to make two side panels and one end panel of the required lengths (see Pleated Dust Ruffle Cut Sizes chart on page 27). Serge or zigzag the seam allowances together and press them to one side.

Step 3. Serge or zigzag-finish the two short ends and one long edge of each ruffle strip. Turn under and press ½ inch at each short edge and topstitch ⅜ inch from the pressed edges. Hem the long finished edge on each panel in the same manner.

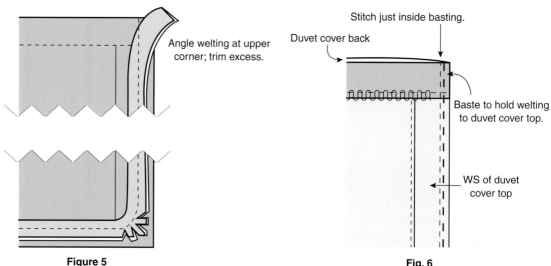

Figure 5
Ease welting around corner; clip as needed.

Angle welting at upper corner; trim excess.

Stitch just inside basting.

Duvet cover back

Baste to hold welting to duvet cover top.

WS of duvet cover top

Fig. 6
Sew duvet cover front and back together.

Step 4. Referring to Figs. 7 and 8, make box and knife-edge pleats in the side and end panels. Reverse the knife-edge pleat positioning on the second side panel to make a mirror-image panel for the opposite side of the bed. Space the two box pleats as desired along the side panel. Press the pleats and machine-baste the layers together at the raw edges.

Step 5. For the dust-ruffle deck, add 1 inch to the width of box spring and ½ inch to the length for seam allowances. Using the upper finished edge of the flat sheet as the upper finished edge of the deck, cut a rectangle from the sheet to match these dimensions. Round the lower corners of the deck to match the corner shape of the box springs.

Step 6. With right sides together and raw edges even, pin the side dust ruffle panels to the deck. They will extend around the corner onto the end of the deck. In the same manner, pin the end ruffle panel to the deck, overlapping the side panels at the corners. Stitch the ruffle panels to the deck. Press the seam allowances toward the deck. When completed and on the bed, the side ruffle panels will overlap the end panels at the corners.

MATERIALS

PILLOW SHAM
Note: *All yardage is for 54-inch-wide decorator fabric. The yardage given for Print #1 and Print #3 and the coordinating solid is adequate for all three common pillow sizes: Standard, 20 x 26 inches; Queen,*

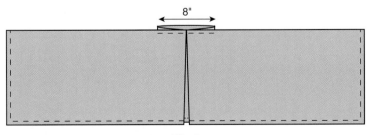

Fig. 7
Reverse the 1" and 4" knife pleats
for the opposite side of bed.

Fig. 8
Pleated End Ruffle

20 x 30 inches; King, 20 x 38 inches.

- 5/8 yard Print #1 for the center panel
- 1 yard Print #3 for the border and back
- 5/8 yard coordinating solid for welting
- Jumbo welting: 3 yards for standard; 3¼ yards for queen; 3⅝ yards for king
- Zipper foot
- Basic sewing supplies and tools

INSTRUCTIONS
Pillow Sham
Project Note: *Use ½-inch-wide seam allowances throughout. Sew all seams with right sides together. Refer to the chart on page 27 for the cutting dimensions for your pillow size.*

Step 1. Referring to the cutting chart, cut the required pieces from each fabric for your pillow sham size.

Step 2. Sew the side border strips to the short edges of the center panel. Press the seams toward the borders. Add the remaining border strips and press toward the borders as shown in Fig. 9.

Step 3. Serge or zigzag-finish one 22-inch-long edge of each back panel rectangle. Turn under and press ½ inch and topstitch ⅜ inch from the folded edge. With right sides together, position the back panels on the front panel with the finished edges overlapping in the center as shown in Fig. 10. Pin the back panels together along the overlapped edge, remove from the front panel and set aside.

Step 4. Make covered welting for the sham as shown in Steps 7 and 8 for the duvet cover. Beginning at the center of one long edge of the sham and rounding the corners as you reach them, pin the welting to the pillow sham front with right sides together and raw edges even. Clip the welting seam allowance as needed to ease it around the corners. Begin stitching 2 inches from the beginning of the welting and end the stitching 4–6 inches from where the welting started as shown in Fig. 11. Remove from the machine.

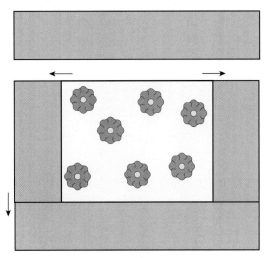

Fig. 9
Press seams in direction of arrows.

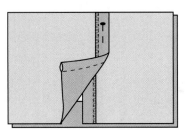

Fig. 10
Position back panels on front panel.
Pin overlapped edges together.

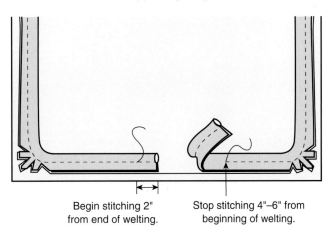

Begin stitching 2" from end of welting.

Stop stitching 4"–6" from beginning of welting.

Fig. 11
Join welting ends.

Step 5. To join the welting ends, remove 3 inches of stitching at the long loose end of the welting so you can fold the bias strip back to avoid cutting it. Cut the welting even with the beginning end. Trim the excess bias, leaving 1 inch beyond the cut end for turn-under allowance and overlap. Turn under ½ inch of the bias at the cut end and wrap the turned edge back over both cut ends of the welting. Complete the stitching as shown in Fig. 12.

Step 6. With right sides together, sew the sham back to the sham front. Remove the pins and turn right side out through the center back opening; press as needed along the welting. ■

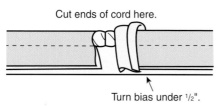

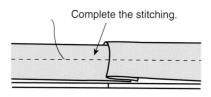

Cut ends of cord here.

Turn bias under ½".

Complete the stitching.

Fig. 12
Butt cord ends and cover with welting fabric.

Duvet Cover Cut Sizes

	Twin	Double	Queen	King
	W x L	W x L	W x L	W x L
Comforter Size	60" x 90"	84" x 90"	90" x 95"	106" x 98"
Duvet Cover Cut Size*	61" x 96"	85" x 95"	91" x 100"	107" x 103"

*Cut sizes include ½" seam allowances on three edges and a 4½" hem allowance at upper edge.

Pillow Sham Cut Sizes

		Double	Queen	King
		W x L	W x L	W x L
Pillow Size		20" x 26"	20" x 30"	20" x 38"
	No. to cut			
Fabric #1				
Center panel	1	14" x 20"	14" x 22"	14" x 30"
Fabric #3				
Side borders	2	5" x 14"	5" x 14"	5" x 14"
Top & bottom borders	2	5" x 28"	5" x 30"	5" x 38"
Back	2	18" x 22"	20" x 22"	25" x 22"

Pleated Dust Ruffle Cut Sizes*

		Twin	Double	Queen	King
		W x L	W x L	W x L	W x L
Box Springs Dimensions		39" x 75"	54" x 75"	60" x 80"	78" x 80"
	No. to cut				
End Panel Cut Size	1	15" x 58"	15" x 73"	15" x 79"	15" x 97"
Side Panel Cut Size	2	15" x 120"	15" x 120"	15" x 125"	15" x 125"

*Based on 14"-long finished skirt drop.

Crazy-Patch Throw

One could only anticipate sweet dreams when napping under this soft, delicate throw.

DESIGN BY MARIAN SHENK

PROJECT SPECIFICATIONS

Skill Level: Beginner

Throw Size: 40 x 48 inches

MATERIALS

- ½ yard each of 4 different colors of 60-inch-wide fleece
- 1¼ yards 60-inch-wide coordinating fleece for backing
- All-purpose thread to match fabrics
- Scraps of lace trim totaling approximately 15 yards
- Basic sewing supplies and tools

INSTRUCTIONS

Step 1. Cut coordinating backing fleece into 42 x 50-inch rectangle.

Step 2. From the darkest ½-yard piece of fleece, cut and join enough 2-inch-wide strips to make 5¼ yards of binding.

Step 3. Starting at one corner, cut a patch from one of the four ½-yard pieces of fleece and pin it to the wrong side of one corner of the backing rectangle.

Step 4. Continue cutting a variety of shapes from the ½-yard pieces of fleece, fitting them together as a puzzle and matching all edges. See the photo for ideas. Baste or pin all of the pieces to the backing until the entire surface is covered.

Step 5. Choose a wide decorative stitch on your machine and stitch over all raw edges where the pieces fit together.

Step 6. Cut and stitch lace trim in place at each seam as shown in the photo. Press as needed, and then trim the patchwork panel to 40 x 48 inches.

Step 7. Pin the binding strip from step 2 to the right side of the patchwork with right sides together and raw edges aligned. Stitch ½ inch from the raw edges.

Step 8. Wrap the binding strip over the raw edge to the back of the throw and pin in place. From the right side, stitch in the ditch of the seam. Trim the excess binding close to the stitching on the back of the completed throw. ∎

Diamond Suede Quilt

This novel quilt is made by appliquéing diamonds on large suede pieces. The method is an easy way to get started sewing with real suede and the results are truly unique.

DESIGN BY PATRICIA CONVERSE

PROJECT SPECIFICATIONS
Skill Level: Intermediate
Quilt Size: Approximately 50 x 50 inches

MATERIALS
Note: *Leather is sold by the square foot. A pigskin suede skin averages about 12 square feet (since all pigs are not the same size). When visiting a leather store, take a tape measure along to be sure the quilt pieces required can be cut from the skins available. When ordering pigskin online, remember skins are irregular in shape. The square footage includes the entire skin and you won't be able to use all of it. The large quilt pieces must be cut from the skin center so you may need two skins each of the gold and ivory to cut the large pieces required. Use rotary cutting tools for the cleanest most accurate cuts. If you do not have this equipment, be sure to purchase a rotary ruler with a 60-degree angle line.*

- 8 x 18-inch rectangle purple pigskin suede
- 12 x 18-inch rectangle forest green pigskin suede
- 12 x 12-foot minimum of gold pigskin suede
- 12 x 12-foot minimum of ivory pigskin suede
- 3 yards 44-inch-wide, or 2 yards 60-inch-wide backing fabric
- 52 x 52-inch square thin batting
- 1 yard lightweight fusible interfacing
- 6 yards ¼-inch-wide corded piping trim
- Leather sewing machine needle, size 16 or 18
- Hand-sewing needle
- All-purpose sewing thread
- Heavy-duty size 40 thread for quilting (optional)
- Rubber cement or Quilter's Choice Basting Glue
- Rotary cutter, mat and ruler
- White tissue paper or tear-away stabilizer
- Masking tape
- Safety pins
- Paper clips
- Press cloth and iron
- Ballpoint pen
- Permanent acid-free marker
- Walking foot, or even-feed foot (optional)
- Basic sewing supplies and tools

INSTRUCTIONS
Project Note: *Read all instructions before beginning. Practice all techniques on samples before working on the quilt. Wash, dry and press the backing fabric before cutting. Preshrink interfacing before cutting as directed by the manufacturer. Cut the interfacing strips along the least stretchy edge,*

usually lengthwise. Always mark leather on the wrong side. A ballpoint pen works well. Always cut leather in a single layer. Stitch test samples on scrap suede before stitching on the quilt pieces. Use a stitch length of 7–10 stitches per inch with all-purpose thread in the needle and on the bobbin. Shorter stitches will tear the leather. Always test the stitching on scraps to determine the proper tension. Use a longer stitch length with heavier thread.

To avoid tearing the leather, never backstitch seams. Instead, knot the thread at the beginning and end of all seams. Stitch only once to avoid weakening the leather with multiple needle holes. Use paper clips instead of straight pins to hold the pieces together for sewing. If the feed dogs mar the suede or if it does not slide easily on the throat plate, place tissue paper or tear-away stabilizer between the machine and the leather project; remove after stitching.

Use a walking foot or even-feed foot to keep layers from creeping while sewing. Finger-press all seams open and roll them with a clean rolling pin for a sharper press. After finger pressing, weight seams with books to

further flatten the seams if needed. Apply rubber cement to the underside of the seam allowance to hold seam allowances in place on the wrong side.

Use a ¼-inch-wide seam allowance throughout this project.

Step 1. From the ivory suede, cut one 30½-inch center square and four 10½-inch corner squares. From the gold suede, cut four border strips, each 10½ x 30½ inches.

Step 2. Using a rotary cutter, mat and ruler, cut one 3¼ x 16¾-inch strip from the purple suede and from the gold suede. Cut four strips from the forest green strip. Using the 60-degree-angle line on the ruler, cut four 60-degree diamonds from each strip as shown in Fig. 1. You should have four purple, four gold and 12 forest green diamonds.

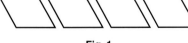

Fig. 1
Cut four 60-degree diamond shapes from each strip.

Step 3. From the interfacing, cut 18 strips, each ½ x 36 inches.

Step 4. If using 44-inch-wide backing fabric, cut it into two equal lengths. Trim away the selvages on both pieces. With right sides facing, sew the lengths together lengthwise. Press the seam open.

Step 5. For the diamond placement on the ivory center square, mark 16 radials by folding the leather with right sides together and finger pressing the fold lines. First fold the square in half, top to bottom. Finger-press and open. Fold the square in half again, side to side. Finger-press and open. Fold square in half, diagonally, finger-press and open. Repeat on the opposite diagonal. You should have eight segments marked by folds. Next, fold each segment in half, fold line to fold line. Finger-press and open. Arrange the colored diamond shapes on the fold lines as shown in Fig. 2.

Fig. 2
Appliqué placement for center square.

Step 6. Remove diamonds one by one and apply a light coat of rubber cement or basting glue to the wrong side. Reposition and smooth into place. Allow the glue to dry, and then edgestitch each diamond in place. Pull threads to the back and knot.

Step 7. Fold each ivory corner square in half diagonally with right sides together. Finger-press and open. Repeat with the opposite corners. Apply rubber cement or glue to the wrong side of a forest green diamond and center on the ivory square, using the creases as positioning guides. Smooth into place, allow to dry and edgestitch in place. Pull threads to the back and knot.

Step 8. Apply fusible interfacing strips to the wrong side of the quilt top along all outer edges. Use a press cloth to protect the leather and fuse in place following the manufacturer's directions.

Step 9. Using paper clips in place of straight pins, paper-clip a gold border strip to opposite edges of the center ivory square with right sides together. Stitch, removing the paper clips before you reach them. ***Note***: *Do not stitch over the paper clips.* Finger-press the seams open. Knot the threads at the ends of each seam.

Step 10. With right sides together, paper-clip an ivory square to each end of the remaining gold border strips. ***Note***: *Make sure to position the ivory squares so that the long points of the diamonds point to the center of the large ivory square as shown in Fig. 3.* Sew together. Finger-press seams open. Knot threads at the seam ends.

Step 11. With right sides together, paper-clip and stitch the quilt sections, as shown in Fig. 3. Finger-press the seams open. Knot threads at the seam ends.

Step 12. For a label, cut a diamond or other shape from a scrap of the suede. With an acid-free, permanent marking pen, sign your name on the smooth side of the suede. Glue the label to the right side of the quilt backing in the lower left or right corner, being careful to place it at least ½ inch from the raw edges. Allow glue to dry. Topstitch the label in place.

QUILT ASSEMBLY

Note: Do not stretch any of the layers when placing together.

Step 1. On a large table or the floor, place the backing right side down and smooth out any wrinkles. Use wide masking tape to hold it in place.

Step 2. Lay the batting on top of the backing and smooth out any wrinkles. Secure the batting with masking tape.

Step 3. Lay the quilt top right side up on top of the batting. Smooth out any wrinkles and use masking tape to secure it. Carefully trim the batting and backing even with the quilt-top edges. Remove the tape.

Step 4. Remove the quilt top and baste the batting to the backing.

Step 5. Position the corded piping in the seam allowance on the right side of the quilt top, rounding the corners. Overlap the piping ends and angle them toward the outer edge where they meet as shown in Fig. 4. Using a zipper foot and basting-length stitch, baste the piping in place. Trim corners.

Step 6. With right sides together, paper-clip the backing/batting sandwich to the quilt top. Using the zipper foot, stitch the layers together, leaving a 10- to 12-inch opening for turning. Finger-press the seams open. Turn the quilt right side out through the opening. Blind-stitch the opening closed.

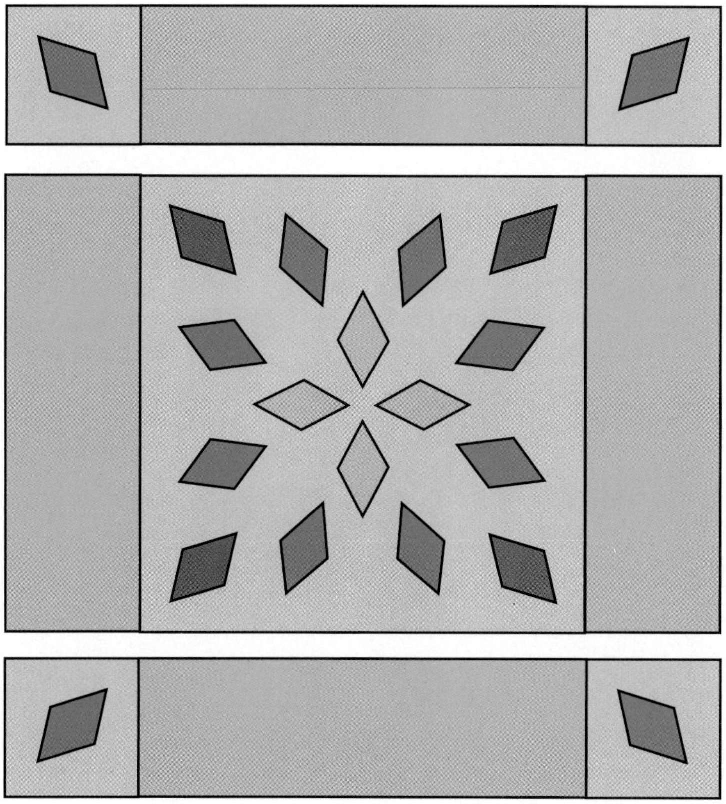

QUILTING

Note: Simple and sparse quilting is best for suede and leather. Closely spaced stitches and too much quilting will weaken the quilt. Use masking tape or the edge of the presser foot as a guide for stitching. Test masking tape on a scrap to make sure it won't pull away any of the suede nap when you remove it. If you use masking tape, tape only the area where you will be stitching and remove it as soon as you have finished. Do not leave tape on the surface of the skin for extended periods of time to avoid damaging or discoloring the suede nap.

Step 1. Working on a large, flat surface, smooth out the quilt layers and use safety pins to pin-baste the layers together in the seamlines.

Step 2. Machine-quilt. Pull the threads to the back and knot securely. Thread the ends into a needle and slip the needle between the layers to bury them in the quilt for added security. ■

Fig. 3
Sew ivory corner squares to top and bottom border strips.
Sew completed borders to quilt top.

Figure 4
Overlap cording ends.
Trim even with quilt edge.

Vintage Charm Pillows

Add a touch of vintage charm to any room with these pillows. Purchase or search through old costume jewelry for beads or pins to embellish the pillows.

DESIGNS BY PEARL LOUISE KRUSH

PROJECT SPECIFICATIONS
Skill Level: Confident Beginner
Envelope Pillow Size:
Approximately 10 x 12½ inches
Flower Appliqué Pillow Size:
Approximately 8½ x 14 inches

MATERIALS

BOTH PILLOWS
- 1 fat quarter dark print
- 1 fat quarter light yellow print
- 1 fat quarter medium yellow print
- 1 fat quarter stripe print
- Scrap of green print
- 1 yard tassel trim
- 1 yard braided trim
- 1 yard beaded trim or assorted beads
- 1-inch decorative button or pin
- Polyester fiberfill
- All-purpose thread to match fabrics
- Basic sewing supplies and tools

INSTRUCTIONS
Envelope Pillow
Project Note: *Use ¼-inch-wide seam allowances for both pillows.*

Step 1. From the dark print, cut one 10½-inch square for the pillow front. From the medium yellow print, cut one 10½ square for the pillow back. From the stripe, cut one 8½ x 10½-inch rectangle for the flap.

Step 2. If you have a serger, serge finish one long edge of the flap rectangle. Otherwise zigzag finish the edge. Turn the finished edge under ¼ inch and press. Stitch ⅛ inch from the turned edge. Fold the rectangle in half with right sides together and stitch ¼ inch from the short raw edges. Press the seam open and turn right side out. Center the seam on the back of the flap and press as shown in Fig. 1.

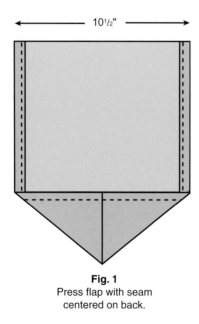

10½"

Fig. 1
Press flap with seam
centered on back.

Step 3. With right sides together, center and pin the flap to one short edge of the pillow back. You should have a ¼-inch-wide seam allowance beyond the outer edges of the flap. Stitch ¼ inch from the raw edges and press the seam toward the flap.

Step 4. With the flap extended, pin the pillow back to the pillow front with right sides together and raw edges even. Stitch ¼ inch from the side and bottom edges. Turn the pillow cover right side out.

Step 5. Pin tassel trim to the flap edge with the trim ends extending ½ inch beyond the flap edges. Turn the trim under at the ends and pin in place. Stitch the trim to the flap. Pin braided trim to the flap ¼ inch above the upper edge of the tassel trim, allowing ½ inch to turn under at each end. Turn ends under, pin and stitch in place.

Step 6. Sew beads or beaded trim in the space between the braid and tassel trims.

Step 7. Stuff the pillow firmly with polyester fiberfill. Fold the flap to the pillow front and sew in place with a button or pin. Hand-tack the flap edges in place on the pillow front.

INSTRUCTIONS
Flower Appliqué Pillow

Step 1. From light yellow print, cut one 9 x 14½-inch rectangle for the pillow front. From the medium yellow print, cut one 9 x 14½-inch rectangle for the pillow back. From the dark print, cut five 2½-inch squares for the flower petals. From the medium yellow print, cut one 1½-inch-diameter circle for the flower center. From the green print, cut one 1¼ x 12-inch true-bias strip for the stem and cut two 2½ squares for the leaves. Cut two 9-inch-long pieces of braided trim and of tassel trim.

Step 2. Fold the dark print squares in half diagonally with wrong sides together. Thread a needle with matching thread and knot the ends together. Hand baste the raw edges together and pull the thread tight to shape the fabric into a petal as shown in Fig. 2. Tie off the threads securely. Set the petal aside. Follow the same procedure to make leaves from the green print squares.

Step 3. For the flower center, thread a needle and knot the ends together. Hand baste around the outer edge of the 1½-inch yellow print circle as shown in Fig. 3. Place a small amount of polyester fiberfill in the center of the circle. Pull the gathering thread tight, encasing the stuffing and take several stitches to secure. Set aside.

Step 4. For the stem, fold the green bias strip in half lengthwise with wrong sides together. Stitch ¼ inch from the long raw edges and trim the seam to ⅛ inch.

Step 5. Center and pin the stem to the pillow front, trimming the stem to end about 4 inches above the lower edge. Stitch in place on top of the existing stitching. Fold the stem over to cover the raw edge and slipstitch the folded edge to the pillow front as shown in Fig. 4.

Step 6. Referring to the photo for placement, pin and hand sew the leaves in place on the stem.

Step 7. Position the flower petals at the upper end of the stem

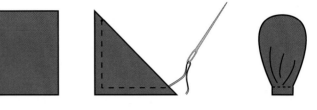

Fig. 2
Hand baste and pull thread to gather fabric into petals and leaves.

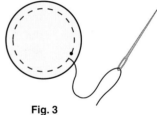

Fig. 3
Hand baste around outer edge.

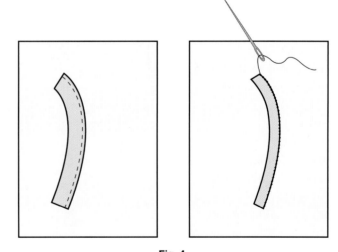

Fig. 4
Sew stem in place, then fold over raw edge and hand sew in place.

and sew in place. Add a yellow print center and sew in place with matching thread.

Step 8. Pin and sew the braided trim to the pillow front, 1 inch below the upper raw edge and 3 inches above the bottom raw edge. Pin and sew the tassel trim ¼ inch below each row of braided trim.

Step 9. With right sides together, pin and sew the pillow front to the pillow back. Leave a 5-inch opening on one long edge for turning.

Step 10. Turn the pillow cover right side out and stuff firmly with polyester fiberfill. Whipstitch the opening closed.

Step 11. To finish, sew beaded trim or assorted beads in the space between the braided and tassel trims at the top and bottom edges of the pillow. ■

Simply Floral, Simply Round

Decorator pillows are a wonderful way to brighten a room setting with a minimal investment of time and money. Choose coordinating fabrics that complement your decor for these two easy-to-sew pillows.

DESIGNS BY JULIE WEAVER

PROJECT SPECIFICATIONS
Skill Level: Confident Beginner
Pillow With Flange Size: 18 inches square, including flange
Round Pillow Size: 12 inches in diameter

MATERIALS
Note: *Yardage given is for 54-inch-wide decorator fabrics and is enough for both pillows. Make one of each or make a pair of one style in fabrics and colors that suit your decorating scheme.*

- ²/₃ yard large floral print
- ²/₃ yard small floral print
- 1½ yards coordinating trim for flange pillow
- 12-inch square pillow form for flange pillow
- 12-inch-diameter bowl or plate for pattern for round pillow
- Water- or air-soluble marking pen
- Pinking shears
- Polyester fiberfill for round pillow
- Two 1½-inch-diameter covered-button forms for round pillow
- Scrap of lightweight fusible interfacing
- Button and carpet thread for round pillow

- All-purpose thread to match fabrics
- Basic sewing supplies and tools

INSTRUCTIONS
Simply Floral Pillow With Flange
Project Note: *Use ½-inch-wide seam allowances and stitch all seams with right sides together.*

Step 1. From the small floral print, cut one 19-inch square for the pillow front. From the large floral print, cut one 13-inch square for the pillow front inset and two 10 x 19-inch pieces for the pillow back.

Step 2. Fold the 19-inch square in fourths with right sides together and press lightly to mark the center. On the wrong side of the square, draw a 12-inch square in the center as shown in Fig. 1.

Step 3. Machine-stitch on the marked lines and cut out the center ½ inch inside the stitching. Clip to the corners as shown in Fig. 2.

Step 4. Using the stitching as your guide, turn under and press

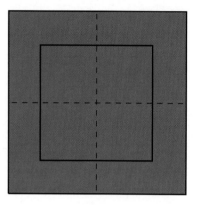

Fig. 1
Draw a 12" square in the center of the 19" square.

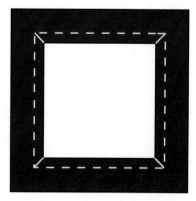

Fig. 2
Cut out center ½" from stitching; clip to corners.

the ½-inch allowance around the opening.

Step 5. Center the 13-inch square of large floral print for the front inset under the opening. Pin in place and edgestitch the opening edges to the square as shown in Fig. 3.

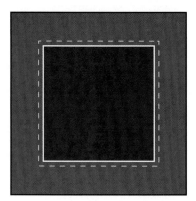

Fig. 3
Stitch turned inner edge to pillow front insert.

Step 6. With right sides together, stitch two 10 x 19-inch backing strips together as shown in Fig. 4, backstitching and changing to a basting-length stitch for the center 12 inches. Press the seam open. Topstitch ¼ inch from the seam line on each side as shown in Fig. 5. **Note:** *You will remove the basting later.*

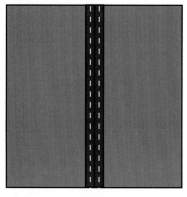

Fig. 5
Topstitch ¼" from seam line.

Step 7. With right sides together, pin the pillow front to the back. Stitch ½ inch from all raw edges. Clip across the corners. Clip the basting in the center of the pillow-back seam; remove the stitches. Turn the pillow cover right side out through the opening. Press the outer edges.

Step 8. To attach the pillow front and back, stitch through all layers on top of the previous stitching that frames the large floral center.

Step 9. Beginning in the center of one side of the pillow cover, position coordinating trim along the stitching around the pillow center. Turn under the end and overlap where it meets the beginning. Stitch in place.

Step 10. Insert the pillow form through the center-back opening and invisibly slipstitch the opening edges together as shown in Fig. 6. Use a doubled thread for added security.

INSTRUCTIONS
Simply Round Pillow
Project Note: *Use ½-inch-wide seam allowances and stitch all seams with right sides together.*

Step 1. Cut a 13½-inch square from the large floral print and from the small floral print. Pin the squares together with right sides facing and raw edges aligned.

Step 2. Position the 12-inch-diameter bowl or plate in the center of the layered squares and trace around it using the marking pen. Remove the bowl.

Step 3. Stitch on the marked line, leaving a 2-inch-long opening for turning. Cut out the pillow ½ inch from the stitching, using pinking shears to trim the edges of the seam and notch out the fullness at the same time as shown in Fig. 7. Turn right side out and press.

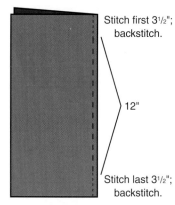

Fig. 4
Baste center 12".

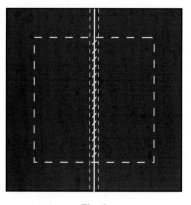

Fig. 6
Slipstitch edges together.

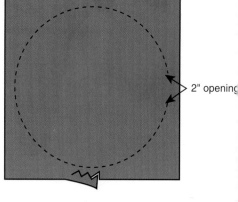

Fig. 7
Cut out circle with pinking shears.

Step 4. Stuff the pillow cover firmly with polyester fiberfill. Use small handfuls and open and fluff the fibers before inserting to avoid lumps. Smooth and round the edges of the pillow as you stuff the pillow cover. Hand-stitch the opening closed.

Step 5. Cover the buttons following the package directions. Cover one with the large floral and one with the small floral print. To prevent the button forms from showing through the fabric, back the fabric circles with lightweight fusible interfacing before you cover the forms.

Step 6. Thread a long needle with button and carpet thread and knot the end securely. Insert the needle in the pillow center and draw through to the opposite side. Pull the thread tight to make an indentation in the pillow center. Reinsert the needle and bring to the top of the pillow. Take several tight stitches through the pillow center to secure the indentation. Attach buttons of the opposite prints to each side of the finished pillow. ■

It's a Wrap

Make a drawstring-shirred fabric wrap for a potted plant or an oversize candle. A pretty print lining peeks out at the edge of this versatile drawstring pouch.

DESIGN BY JULIE WEAVER

PROJECT SPECIFICATIONS

Skill Level: Beginner
Wrap Size: 18-inch-diameter circle when opened flat; will fit around a potted plant or large candle

MATERIALS

- 5/8 yard 44/45- or 54-inch-wide crushed panné velvet (bag)
- 5/8 yard 44/45-inch-wide cotton print (lining)
- 1 yard ¼-inch-diameter cord (drawstring)
- All-purpose sewing thread to match fabrics
- Water- or air-soluble marking pen
- Pencil, string and a 19-inch square of tissue paper to make a pattern
- Pinking shears
- Liquid seam sealant
- Basic sewing supplies and tools

INSTRUCTIONS

Step 1. To make a pattern for the circle, fold the tissue paper square in half and then in half again, keeping all cut edges even. Tie a string to the eraser end of the pencil. Measure 9 inches from the pencil and mark the string. Place the mark at the folded corner of the square and draw an arc as shown in Fig. 1. Cut along the line and open out to an 18-inch circle.

Step 2. Cut a 19-inch square from the lining and from the panné velvet. Pin the pattern to the wrong side of the lining and trace around the outer edge. Remove the pattern.

Step 3. Pin the two fabric squares together with right sides facing. Stitch on the drawn line, leaving a 2-inch opening for turning as shown in Fig. 2.

Step 4. Using pinking shears, cut out the circle ⅜ inch from the stitching. The pinking automatically notches out fullness in the curved edge so the finished edge turns more smoothly. Turn the circle right side out through the opening and press from the lining side to avoid damaging the velvet. Slipstitch the opening edges together.

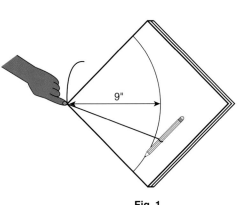

Fig. 1
Hold string taut at folded corner.

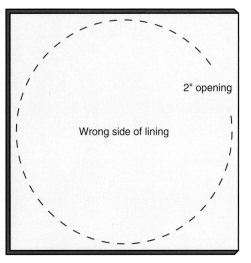

Fig. 2
Stitch on drawn line.

Step 5. To make the casing, topstitch 2 inches from the outer finished edge of the circle. Stitch again ½ inch from the first stitching (1½ inches from the outer edge). On the velvet side of the circle, make a slit in the casing for the cord as shown in Fig. 3. Treat the cut edges with liquid seam sealant and allow to dry.

Step 6. Thread the cord through the casing. Finish the cord ends by tying an overhand knot in each one and allowing the ends to untwist. Tuck a potted plant, large candle or other gift goodies inside and tie the cord in a knot. ■

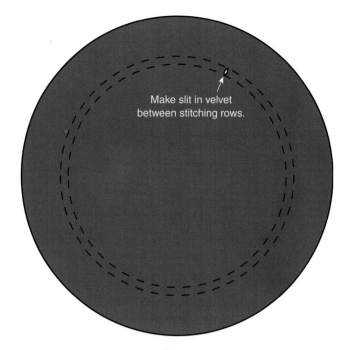

Make slit in velvet between stitching rows.

Fig. 3
Topstitch 1½" and 2" from outer finished edge.

Tulip Tablecloth

A simple purchased tablecloth is the perfect backdrop for a border of pretty tulips. Rotary-cutting tools make it easy to cut perfect diamonds for the leaves and petals. Fusing and zigzagging hold the flowers in place.

DESIGN BY JUDITH SANDSTROM

PROJECT SPECIFICATIONS
Skill Level: Beginner
Tablecloth Size: 52 x 70 inches

MATERIALS
Note: *Materials listed are for 44/45-inch-wide tone-on-tone cotton prints.*

- Purchased 52 x 70-inch tablecloth with at least 50 percent polyester fiber content
- ¼ yard rose print for outer petals
- ¼ yard green print for leaves
- ¼ yard pink print for center petals
- 1¼ yards paper-backed fusible web
- Water- or air-soluble marking pen
- All-purpose thread to match fabrics
- Rotary cutter, mat and ruler
- Iron
- Sewing machine with zigzag stitch
- Basic sewing supplies and tools

INSTRUCTIONS
Step 1. Prewash the tablecloth and press to remove wrinkles. Prewash all three print fabrics for the flower appliqués. Press.

Step 2. From the fusible web and the rose fabric, cut two 9 x 17-inch strips. Following manufacturer's directions, apply the fusible web to the wrong side of each rose strip.

Step 3. With the rose strips right sides together on the rotary-cutting mat, cut a total of eight strips, each 1¾ inches wide.

Step 4. With the strip pairs perfectly aligned on the cutting mat, make 45-degree-angle cuts along the length of the strip. Space the cuts 1¾ inches apart to cut sets of perfect diamonds as shown in Fig. 1. You need a total of 24 sets (48 diamonds) for the tulip petals.

Step 5. For the leaves, cut two 6 x 17-inch strips each fusible web and green print. Apply the fusible web to the wrong side of each piece of green print. With raw edges even and right sides together, position the green fused strips on the cutting mat as you did for the outer tulip petals in Step 3. Cut a total of four 1¾-inch-wide strips from the green print. From the strip sets, cut a total of 10 sets of 1¾-inch diamonds (20 diamonds total). From the remaining fabric, cut 10 strips each ¼ x 3½ inches for the stems.

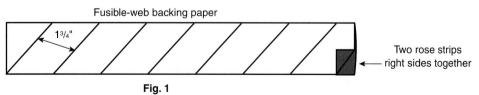

Fig. 1
Cut 6 diamond pairs from each 2-strip set.

Step 6. From the pink print and the fusible web, cut two strips each 6 x 17 inches. Apply the fusible web to the wrong side of each piece of pink. Layer the pieces with right sides together and cut a total of four strips, each 2½ x 17 inches. Cut a total of 24 (2½-inch) squares from the fusible-backed strips as shown in Fig. 2.

Step 7. Remove the paper backing from each of the fusible-backed squares and diamonds.

Step 8. Mark the center at each finished edge of the tablecloth with a pin or water- or air-soluble marking pen.

Step 9. Working on one edge at a time with the tablecloth on a large flat surface, arrange the diamonds and squares to create the tulips as shown in Fig. 3. Place the lower edges of the appliqués 1¼ inches from the tablecloth finished edge. Use straight pins to hold motifs in position until you have finalized

the arrangement. Fuse in place following the manufacturer's directions. Repeat along the remaining edges of the tablecloth.

Step 10. Adjust the machine for a short, narrow zigzag stitch. Using thread on the top of the machine to match the fabric color, zigzag along each raw edge of each motif as shown in Fig. 4. Begin with the green leaves and stems. Next, stitch the pink squares and finish with the rose diamonds. ■

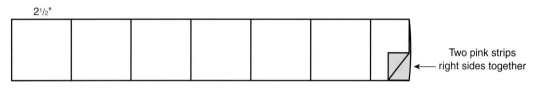

Fig. 2
Cut 6 pairs of squares from each 2-strip set.

Mark centers on each edge.

Fig. 3
Tulip Tablecloth Diagram

Fig. 4
Zigzag all edges of each appliqué.

Reversible Table Runners

Mix luxurious decorator fabrics with trim and tassels to stitch up these elegant runners for your dining or occasional table.

DESIGNS BY CAROL ZENTGRAF

PROJECT SPECIFICATIONS

Skill Level: Confident beginner
Tasseled Patchwork Table Runner Size: 15 x 70 inches, excluding tassels
Bordered Table Runner Size: 16½ x 82 inches, excluding tassels

MATERIALS

TASSELED PATCHWORK TABLE RUNNER

Note: *Materials listed are for 54/60-inch-wide decorator fabrics.*

- 1¼ yards coordinating tone-on-tone stripe for runner front
- ½ yard damask or tapestry-like fabric for runner front
- 1½ yards coordinating small motif jacquard fabric for runner back
- 2½ yards ¼-inch-diameter corded piping
- ½ yard gimp trim to coordinate with the runner back fabric
- 1 drapery tie-back with two tassels
- 1²/₃ yards 18-inch-wide, shirtweight fusible interfacing
- Water- or air-soluble marking pen
- All-purpose thread to match fabric
- Double-sided basting tape
- Permanent fabric adhesive
- Zipper foot
- Basic sewing supplies and tools

INSTRUCTIONS

Tasseled Patchwork Table Runner

Project Note: Use ½-inch wide seam allowances. Stitch all seams with right sides together.

Step 1. From the tone-on-tone stripe, cut one piece 16 x 29 inches along the lengthwise grain so the stripes run along the length of the piece. Cut one 8-inch x fabric-width strip. From this strip, cut two pieces, each 8 x 16 inches.

Step 2. From the damask for the runner front, cut two 13 x16-inch pieces for the points and two strips each 3 x 16 inches. From the fabric for the back, cut two strips each 16 x 36 inches.

Step 3. Cut and apply interfacing to the wrong side of each piece of damask and tone-on-tone stripe following the manufacturer's directions.

Step 4. Referring to Fig. 1, mark and cut a 45-degree-angle point at one long edge of each 8 x 16-inch damask rectangle. Repeat at one short end of each 16 x 36-inch strip for the back.

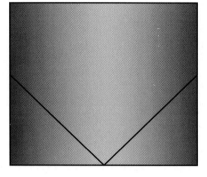

Fig. 1
Mark and cut 45-degree-angle points.

Step 5. Using double-sided basting tape to hold it in place, position a 16-inch-long piece of corded piping at each long edge of the 3 x 16-inch damask strips and along the long, straight edge of each pointed panel as shown in Fig. 3. Sew a 3 x 16-inch piped strip to each short end of the 16 x 29-inch striped panel (see photo).

Step 6. Sew an 8 x 16-inch striped panel to each pointed panel. Referring to the photo, sew the resulting pieces to opposite ends of the runner to complete the assembly. Use the zipper foot to stitch as close to the corded piping as possible. Press the seams toward the strips and the pointed ends.

Step 7. At one short end of one of the backing strips, turn under and

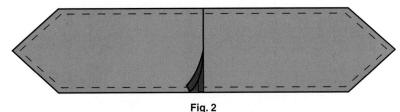

Fig. 2
Lap backing over folded edge.

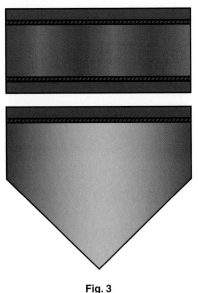

Fig. 3
Use basting tape to position
corded piping on runner pieces.

press 1 inch. Pin the piece to the runner front with right sides together. Pin the remaining runner in place, overlapping the turned edge at the center. Referring to Fig. 2, stitch ½ inch from all edges, changing to a short stitch length for 1 inch on each side of the points. Take a few stitches across the point (see Tasseled Valance Panels, Fig. 4 on page 60). Trim the seam to ¼ inch and clip the points. Turn right side out through the center opening and press. Use a ½-inch-wide strip of fusible web to fuse the opening closed. Disguise the fused edge by gluing gimp trim in place on the runner back, turning under the raw edges even with the finished runner edges.

Step 8. Cut the drapery tieback into two equal lengths. On each end of the runner make a 2½-inch-diameter circle of permanent fabric adhesive. Beginning in the center of the circle of glue, arrange the tieback cord in a tight spiral that ends with the tassel at the base. Allow to dry.

MATERIALS

BORDERED TABLE RUNNER
Note: *Materials listed are for 54/60-inch-wide decorator fabrics.*

- 1⅔ yards damask or tapestry-like fabric for the runner center
- 1¼ yards coordinating solid decorator fabric for the runner back
- ½ yard 60-inch-wide* tone-on-tone

stripe for points and borders
- ½-inch-wide fusible web strip
- 1 yard tasseled fringe
- 2 large tassels
- 1⅔ yards 18-inch-wide shirtweight fusible interfacing
- Water- or air-soluble marking pen
- All-purpose thread to match fabric
- Permanent fabric adhesive
- Basic sewing supplies and tools

__Note__: If fabric is only 54 inches wide, purchase an additional ⅛ yard and piece the border strips to the required length (see Step 2).

INSTRUCTIONS
Bordered Table Runner
Project Note: *Use ½-inch-wide seam allowances. Stitch all seams with right sides together.*

Step 1. From the fabric for the runner center, cut one 16 x 59-inch strip, cutting along the lengthwise grain. You will have fabric remaining to use for additional runners or coordinating accessories. From the backing fabric, cut two 17½ x 42-inch strips, cutting along the lengthwise grain.

Step 2. From the tone-on-tone stripe, cut two border strips, each 1¾ x 59 inches. Cut the strips across the stripes along the crosswise grain. Cut one strip 13 inches wide, cutting across the fabric width. From the strip, cut two pieces each 13 x 17½ inches, for the runner points.

Step 3. From the fusible interfacing, cut one 16 x 59-inch strip and apply to the wrong side of the runner center following manufacturer's directions. Cut and fuse interfacing to the wrong side of each 13 x 17½-inch striped piece and to each of the 1¾ x 59-inch striped border strips.

Step 4. Referring to Fig. 1, mark and cut a 45-degree-angle point at one long edge of each 13 x 17½-inch rectangle. Repeat at one short end of each 17½ x 43-inch strip of backing fabric.

Step 5. Sew a striped border strip to each long edge of the runner panel. Press the seams open. Sew a striped point to each short end of the runner; press seams open.

Step 6. At the short end of one of the backing strips, turn under and press 1 inch. Pin the strip to the runner with right sides together. Pin the remaining runner strip in place, overlapping the first at the folded edge. Stitch ½ inch from all edges as shown in Fig. 2. Change to a short stitch (18–20 stitches per inch) for 1 inch on each side of the point (see Tasseled Valance Panels, Fig. 4 on page 60). Take a few stitches across the point rather than stitching to the point and pivoting. Trim the seams to ¼ inch and clip the points. Before turning the runner right side out through the center back opening, snip two stitches at each point to make an opening for the tassel cords. Turn right side out and press. Fuse the opening closed with a ½-inch-wide strip of fusible web.

Step 7. Insert a tassel in the opening at each point, clipping additional stitches only as needed to fit the cords inside. Slipstitch the opening closed, catching the loop in the stitches.

Step 8. Cut the tasseled trim into two equal lengths. Position and glue trim in place, centering it over the seams at each end of the runner. Turn under the raw ends even with the runner edges. Glue in place. ∎

Custom-Fit Table & Chair Covers

Give any table or chair an instant face-lift with a custom-fit slipcover. Coordinating fabrics and sheer ribbon ties dress up this colorful duo—a banded tablecloth for a narrow hall table and a coordinating cover set for a basic straight-back dining chair.

DESIGNS BY CAROL ZENTGRAF

PROJECT SPECIFICATIONS
Skill Level: Intermediate
Table Cover Size: 36½ x 19 x 28-inch finished table cover
Chairback Cover Size: 17 x 19 inches on the chair
Seat Cover Size: 16-inches square with 6-inch-long pleated skirt.
Note: Adjust dimensions and materials to fit your table and chair (see page 54).

MATERIALS

TABLE COVER
Note: Materials listed are for 54/60-inch-wide decorator fabrics.

- 3½ yards large floral print for the top and skirt panels
- 2 1/3 yards coordinating, small all-over print for corner pleats and bottom band
- Water- or air-soluble marking pen
- All-purpose sewing thread to match fabrics
- 4 (7/8-inch-diameter) covered-button forms
- Basic sewing supplies and tools

INSTRUCTIONS
Table Cover
Project Note: Use ½-inch-wide seam allowances throughout. Sew all seams with right sides together.

Step 1. Determine your table measurements by following the directions in Measure Your Table on page 54. Add 1 inch to each measurement for seam allowances.

Step 2. Cut the top panel from the floral print using the measurements determined in Step 1. For the bottom-banded skirt panels, subtract 4 inches from the desired skirt length determined in Step 1. Cut skirt panels for the ends and sides of the tablecloth from the floral print using the adjusted measurements.

Step 3. For the allover print bottom bands, cut two 5-inch-wide strips equal to the table width plus 1 inch for the side skirt panels. Cut two 5-inch-wide strips equal to the table depth plus 1 inch for the end skirt panels.

Step 4. For the allover-print corner pleats, cut four 17-inch-wide panels of the skirt length determined in Step 1.

Step 5. Sew each contrast band to the lower edge of a corresponding skirt panel. Press the seam toward the skirt panel and finish the seam edges together with serging or zigzagging.

Step 6. Fold each contrast pleat panel in half lengthwise and mark the center. Sew a pleat panel to each end of each side skirt panel. Serge or zigzag the seam allowance edges together. Press the seam allowances toward the skirt panels as shown in Fig. 3 on page 55.

Step 7. Serge-finish the lower raw edge of the skirt. Turn under and press ½ inch and topstitch in place 3/8 inch from the turned edge.

Step 8. To form the pleat for each corner, bring the skirt side and end panel edges to the meet in

Measure Your Table

Note: *Refer to Fig. 1 to measure your table for a fitted table cover and determine the panel cut sizes.*

Step 1. For the top panel, measure the width and depth of the table and add 1 inch to each dimension (for ½-inch-wide seam allowances). Cut one panel of this size for the tabletop.

Top panel cut size = width + 1 inch x depth + 1 inch

Step 2. For the skirt panels, measure the table height from the edge to the desired finished length. Add 1 inch (½ inch for a seam and ½ inch for a hem allowance). For the cut size of the side skirt panels, use the cutting dimension for the table width from Step 1. Cut two panels of each.

End skirt cut size = depth + 1 inch x length + 1 inch

Side skirt cut size = width + 1 inch x length + 1 inch

Measure Your Chair

For a standard straight-back chair with a square seat, refer to the following instructions and Fig. 2.

Step 1. Measure the seat. A standard chair cushion is 16 inches square, but your chair seat size may vary. Add 1 inch for seam allowances.

Cushion cut size = seat width + 1 inch x seat depth + 1 inch

Step 2. Measure the chair-back width and add 1 inch for seam allowances. Determine how long you want the cover to drop from the top of the chair back. Add 1 inch for seam allowances.

Back cut size = back width + 1 inch x desired length + 1 inch

Note: *You may cut the back cover in two pieces using the above dimensions, or you can double the desired length and cut one long panel of the determined width + 1.*

Desired length x 2 +1 inch = cut length

Note: *For a chair with a shaped back and seat: Measure the chair seat and back dimensions and draw the shapes on tracing paper.
Add ½-inch-wide seam allowances all around each shape. Cut out the tissue paper shapes to use as patterns.*

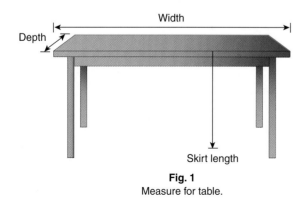

Fig. 1
Measure for table.

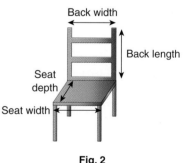

Fig. 2
Measure for chair.

the center of each pleat panel as shown in Fig. 4. Baste the raw edges together at the upper edges of each pleat.

Step 9. Pin the skirt to the top panel with raw edges even. Stitch in place. Press the seam toward the top panel. Serge or zigzag the seam allowance raw edges together.

Step 10. Following the package directions, cover four buttons in the contrasting print. Sew a button in place at each corner to complete the table cover.

MATERIALS

CHAIR COVER SET
Note: *Materials listed are for 54/60-inch-wide decorator fabrics. Directions are for a chair with a 16-inch-square seat and straight back. To adjust cutting dimensions for your chair size and shape, see the chart on page 54.*

- 1¼ yards large floral print
- 1½ yards coordinating, small allover print for contrast bands
- 2½ yards each of two different colors or 5 yards of one color of 3-inch-wide sheer ribbon
- 18 x 18-inch piece of batting
- All-purpose sewing thread to match fabrics
- Temporary spray adhesive (optional)
- Basic sewing supplies and tools

INSTRUCTIONS
Chair Cover Set
Project Note: *Use ½-inch-wide seam allowances throughout. Sew all seams with right sides together.*

Step 1. From the floral print, cut two 18 x 19-inch panels from the floral print for the chair-back cover. For the seat cover, cut two 17-inch floral squares.

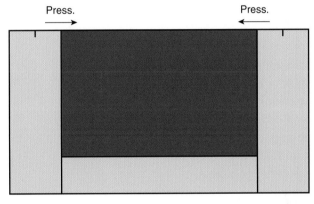

Press. Press.

Fig. 3
Make 2 side panels.

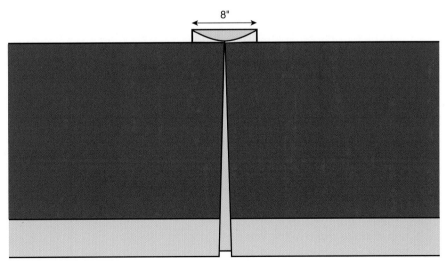

8"

Fig. 4
Form pleats at corners.

Step 2. From the allover print, cut three 2 x 18-inch strips for the contrast bands and one 18 x 40-inch lining panel for the chair back. For the seat cover skirt, cut three 7 x 27-inch strips for the pleated ruffles.

Step 3. Referring to Fig. 5, arrange the floral panels with the 2-inch-wide contrast strips for the chair-back cover and sew together. Press the seams toward the floral panel. Cut four 22½-inch-long strips of ribbon. Center each one at a side edge of a floral panel and baste in place. Pin the loose ribbon ends to the center of each panel to prevent them from getting caught in the seams.

Step 4. With right sides together, stitch the allover print lining panel to the chair-back panel, leaving a 6-inch-long opening in one of the floral panel side edges for turning. Clip the corners to reduce bulk and turn the cover right side out. Press the outer edges and slip-stitch the opening edges together to complete the chair-back cover. Place over the chair back and tie the ribbons into pretty bows at the sides. Cut the ribbon ends at an angle or pink them straight across to finish.

Step 5. Serge-finish one long edge of each 7 x 27-inch strip of allover print. Turn under and press ½ inch and topstitch in place ⅜ inch from the folded edge. At each short edge of each strip, turn under and press ½ inch. Turn under an additional 1 inch and press. Stitch in place close to the inner folded edge as shown in Fig. 6.

Step 6. Fold each strip in half

crosswise to find the center and mark with a pin or a ⅛-inch-long snip. Measure and mark for the pleat fold lines as shown in Fig. 7.

Step 7. Fold pleats in place and press as shown in Fig. 8. Baste the raw edges together to hold pleats in place for stitching.

Press seams in direction of arrows.

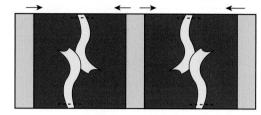

Fig. 5
Baste ribbons in place.

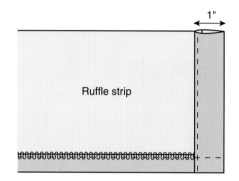

Fig. 6
Stitch edges in place.

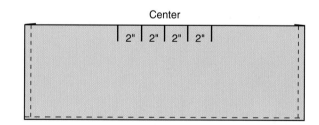

Fig. 7
Make pleat fold lines on ruffle.

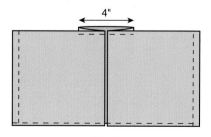

Fig. 8
Make pleat in each ruffle strip.

Step 8. Cut the remaining ribbon into two equal lengths. Fold each piece in half crosswise. Make a pleat in the folded edge of each folded ribbon and pin in place at two opposite corners of one of the floral panels. Baste. Pin the loose ends in the center of the panel as shown in Fig. 9.

Step 9. With raw edges even and right sides together, pin and baste a pleated skirt panel to the side and front edges of the floral panel.

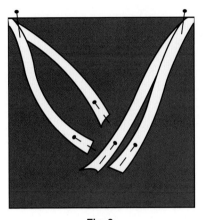

Fig. 9
Pin folded ribbon to opposite corners and center.

Step 10. Baste the batting to the wrong side of the remaining floral square and trim even with the fabric square edges. If desired, use temporary spray adhesive for this step.

Step 11. With right sides together and raw edges even, sew the two floral panels together. Leave a 6-inch-long opening in the back edge for turning. Clip the corners to reduce bulk and turn the cover right side out through the opening. Press. Slipstitch the opening edges together to finish the cover.

Step 12. Position the seat cover on the chair and tie the ribbons into bows around the back posts. Trim the ribbon ends at an angle or pink the edges to finish. ■

Tasseled Valance Panels

Tasseled valances are easy to sew in coordinated cotton prints. Three of them fit a standard window. For larger windows make additional valances, adjusting the panel width as needed for a perfect fit.

DESIGN BY MARIAN SHENK

Skill Level: Beginner

Valance Panel Size: 12½ x 16½ inches, excluding tassels

MATERIALS

THREE VALANCES

- ½ yard large floral print for valance body
- ½ yard coordinating tone-on-tone print for lining
- 4 yards running length of a 1¾-inch-wide border stripe that will finish to 1¼ inches
- All-purpose thread to match fabrics
- 3 tassels, 3 inches long, not including tassel loops
- Basic sewing supplies and tools
- 2-inch-diameter curtain rod

INSTRUCTIONS

Project Note: *Use ¼-inch-wide seam allowances. Stitch all seams with right sides together.*

Step 1. From the floral print, cut three pieces each 10½ x 17 inches. Repeat with the tone-on-tone print for lining.

Step 2. From the border stripe, cut six pieces each 1¾ x 23 inches. Repeat with the tone-on-tone print. Sew a border strip to each long edge of each floral print piece with the excess strip extending beyond one short edge of the panel. Sew a tone-on-tone strip to each long edge of the remaining panels. Press the seams toward the center of each panel.

Step 3. Referring to Fig. 1, cut a 45-degree-angle point at the lower edge of each of the six pieces.

Step 4. Position a tassel at each point on the right side of each floral panel. Baste securely in place as shown in Fig. 2.

Step 5. With right sides together and the tassel inside the layers, sew a tone-on-tone print panel to a floral panel as shown in Fig. 3. Leave an opening for turning in one long edge and change to a shorter stitch length when stitching the 1-inch area on each side of the point. Take two or three stitches across the point rather than pivoting to secure the tassel in the point as shown in Fig. 4. Turn right side out and press. Slipstitch the opening closed.

Step 6. Turn the tabs to the back of the valance with the finished edge even with the upper finished edge of the valance. Slipstitch or machine-edgestitch in place as shown in Fig. 5.

Step 7. Slide the valances over the curtain rod. ■

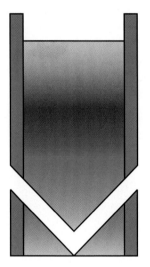

Fig. 1
Cut point at 45-degree angle.
Discard cut-aways.

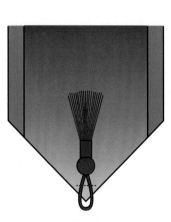

Fig. 2
Baste tassel to point.

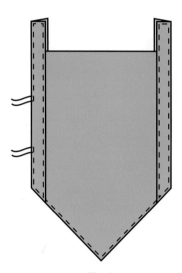

Fig. 3
Leave opening for turning.

Fig. 4
Use smaller stitches on each side of point.
Stitch across point rather than pivoting at point.

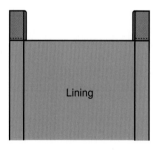

Fig. 5
Stitch tabs in place.

Cheery Yo-Yos Table Set

You will set the table for a delightful tea party for two with this charming project.

DESIGNS BY CHRIS MALONE

PROJECT SPECIFICATIONS

Skill Level: Intermediate
Tea Cozy Size: 11 x 13 inches
Place Mat Size: 12½ x 16½ inches
Napkin Size: 15 inches square
Napkin Ring Size: 2¼ x 4¾ inches

MATERIALS

- 1 yard light green floral print
- ½ yard coordinating dark green floral print
- ⅝ yard coordinating dark rose print
- ¼ yard coordinating medium rose print
- ¼ yard coordinating medium green print
- Assorted scraps of coordinating blues, golds and light rose prints
- 12 x 30-inch rectangle low-loft batting
- 14 x 40-inch rectangle high-loft batting
- 1 yard ivory piping
- 1 yard ivory single-fold bias tape
- Four ⅞-inch ivory buttons
- Eight ⅝-inch ivory buttons
- 11 inches ¾-inch-wide elastic
- All-purpose thread to match fabrics
- Ecru hand-quilting thread (optional)
- Dark green embroidery floss
- Embroidery needle
- Air-soluble marking pen
- Permanent fabric glue
- Zipper foot
- Basic sewing supplies and tools

INSTRUCTIONS

Tea Cozy

Project Note: *Use ¼-inch-wide seam allowances, unless otherwise indicated.*

Step 1. Cut one 11½ x 14-inch rectangle from light green floral print for the tea cozy front. Fold in half so it measures 7 x 11½ inches. Round the corners opposite the fold as shown in Fig. 1. ***Note:*** *A dinner plate is a good guide for this cut.* Using the cozy front as a pattern, cut two more cozy shapes from light green floral print for the lining, one from dark green floral print for the cozy back and two from low-loft batting.

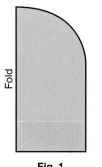

Fig. 1
Round one corner of cozy
as shown.

Step 2. From assorted print scraps, cut two 4½-inch-diameter circles, five 4-inch circles and three 3-inch circles for the yo-yo flowers. From medium green print for the leaves, cut four 4-inch squares, three 3½-inch squares and four 3-inch squares.

Step 3. Referring to the photo, use the air-soluble marking pen to draw freehand lines for vines on the right side of the cozy front. Embroider along the lines with stem stitches, using an embroidery needle and three strands of dark green embroidery floss.

Step 4. Place one cozy lining wrong side up with the batting on top. Smooth the cozy front in place with the right side up. Mark a 2-inch diagonal grid for quilting on the cozy front. Pin and baste the layers together. Prepare the cozy back in the same manner.

Step 5. Quilt on the marked lines by hand or machine.

Step 6. With raw edges even, pin piping to the curved edge of the cozy front. Attach the zipper foot and machine-baste close to the piping cord.

Step 7. Pin the cozy front and back together with right sides facing and raw edges even. Stitching from the wrong side of the cozy front so you can see the basting,

stitch the layers together, positioning the stitches just inside the machine basting. Zigzag- or serge-finish the seam edges together. Turn right side out.

Step 8. Unfold the bias tape and turn under the short end. Beginning in the center of the back raw edge of the cozy, pin the bias to the lower edge of the cozy. Overlap the end when you reach it and trim the excess. Stitch in the fold line. Wrap the bias tape over the raw edge to the inside of the cozy and slipstitch in place.

Step 9. To make a yo-yo flower, finger press a ⅛-inch hem around the outer edge of a fabric circle and hand baste in place. To gather the circle into a flower, draw up the stitches and arrange with the hole in the flower center as shown in Fig. 2. Take several stitches to secure. Make 10 yo-yo flowers.

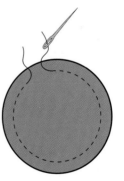

Fig. 2
Make flowers as shown.

Step 10. To make a leaf, fold a fabric square in half, wrong sides together. Fold the corners down to meet in the center with all raw edges even to form a triangle as shown in Fig 3. Hand baste through all layers ⅛ inch from the raw edges. Draw up the thread to

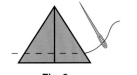

Fig. 3
Make leaves as shown.

gather into a leaf shape. Make 11 leaves.

Step 11. Arrange the flowers along the vines on the tea cozy front and pin in place. Sew yo-yos in place with a button in the center of each one. Use two large buttons for the flowers and small buttons for the remaining flowers.

Step 12. Arrange leaves around flowers as desired with the raw edges under the flower edges. Glue leaves in place under the flowers.

INSTRUCTIONS
Place Mats

Step 1. From the dark green floral print, cut two 8 x 12-inch rect-angles for the center-front panels and two 13 x 17-inch rectangles for the backing. From medium rose print, cut two 3 x 8-inch strips and two 3 x 17-inch strips for the borders. From high-loft batting, cut two 13 x 17-inch rectangles.

Step 2. Sew short border strips to opposite sides of each center panel. Press the seams toward the borders. Add the long border

strips to the center panel and press the seams toward the borders.

Step 3. Arrange a batting rect-angle on the work surface with the backing on top, right side up. Place the place mat front face down on the backing with raw edges even. Pin. Stitch ¼ inch from the raw edges, leaving a 6-inch opening at one edge. Trim the batting close to the stitching and clip the corners. Turn right side out through the opening and press, turning in the opening edg-es. Slipstitch the opening closed.

Step 4. Hand-or machine-quilt by stitching in the ditch of the border seamlines.

INSTRUCTIONS
Napkins

Step 1. From the light green floral print, cut two 15-inch squares. From the dark rose print, cut two 18½-inch squares.

Step 2. Turn under and press ½-inch around each 18½-inch square. Place the squares face down on the work surface and center a green floral square on top of each one with right side up. Pin in place.

Step 3. Turn the napkin square over the green floral square with the folds along the raw edges. Make diagonal folds in the napkin fabric to miter the corners as shown in Fig. 4. Trim excess fabric inside the miter to eliminate bulk. Slipstitch the mitered fold to the napkin at each corner. Machine-stitch close to the inner folded edge of the napkin.

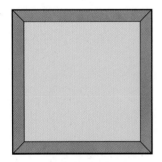

Fig. 4
Miter place mat corners as shown.

INSTRUCTIONS
Napkin Rings

Step 1. From medium green print, cut two 2¼ x 9½-inch strips. Fold each strip in half lengthwise with right sides together and stitch ¼ inch from the long edges. Press the seams open and turn tubes right side out. Center the seams on the back of the tubes and press.

Step 2. Insert a 5½-inch-long piece of elastic into each tube, gathering the tube on the elastic so the ends are even with the tube raw edges. Pin. Fold the tube in half with the seamed side inside and stitch the short ends together. Press the seam open.

Step 3. Make two large yo-yo flowers and four large leaves following the directions in Steps 9-10 for the Tea Cozy.

Step 4. For each napkin ring, sew a ⅞-inch ivory button to the center of a flower and then to the elasticized band, covering the seam. Apply glue to the gathered end of each leaf and tuck under a flower on each side with the leaves parallel to the elastic band (see photo). ■

Checkerboard Kitchen Collection

Choose print coordinates in a complementary color scheme like the one shown to create a French Country quilted table covering and matching Casserole Carrier. Patchwork leftovers are the perfect embellishment for coordinating kitchen towels.

DESIGNS BY PEARL LOUISE KRUSH

PROJECT SPECIFICATIONS

Skill Level: Confident beginner to intermediate

Table Cover Size: 60 square inches

Casserole Carrier Size: Fits a 9 x 13-inch baking pan

Towel Size: 18 x 24 inches

MATERIALS

QUILTED PATCHWORK TABLE COVER

All yardage is for 44/45-inch-wide cotton fabric.

- 1¼ yards red large floral print for the center panel and outer border
- 1 yard green tone-on-tone print for the center panel and binding
- ¾ yard red and cream paisley print for inner border
- ¾ yard coordinating red stripe for the middle border
- ²/₃ yard small red-on-cream floral print for the Nine-Patch blocks and checkerboards for outer borders
- ²/₃ yard red small floral print for the Nine-Patch blocks and checkerboard for outer borders
- 3¾ yards backing fabric in coordinating print
- 64-inch square thin cotton batting or 4 yards of 44/45-inch-wide cotton flannel
- Basic sewing supplies

INSTRUCTIONS

Quilted Patchwork Table Cover

Project Note: *Use ¼-inch-wide seam allowances throughout. Sew all seams with right sides together. Press as directed by the arrows.*

Step 1. From the large floral print, cut one 12½-inch square for the center block and four strips each 6½ x 36½ inches for the outer border.

Step 2. From the green tone-on-tone print, cut two strips each 6½ x 44 inches; from these strips, cut four 6½ x 12½-inch pieces for the center panel. Cut seven 2½ x 44-inch binding strips.

Step 3. From the paisley print, cut four 6½ x 44-inch strips; from these strips, cut four 6½ x 24½-inch strips for the inner border.

Step 4. From the stripe, cut four strips each 6½ x 36½ inches for the middle border.

Step 5. From the red-on-cream print, cut eight strips each 2½ x 44 inches. From the red small floral print, cut eight strips each 2½ x 44 inches. Cut each strip in half crosswise for a total of 16 strips of each color.

Step 6. Using the strips from Step 5, make five strip units using two red-on-cream floral strips and

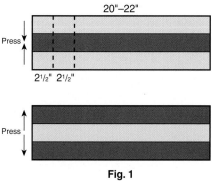

Fig. 1
Make 5 of each strip unit.
Cut 36 segments of each color combination.

1 red small floral strip in each as shown in Fig. 1. Press the seams toward the red small floral strip in each unit. From the units, cut a total of 36 (2½-inch-wide) segments. Using the remaining strips, make five units using two red strips and one white strip in each. Press the seams toward the red strips in each unit. Crosscut 36 (2½-inch-wide) segments. **Note:** *You will have extra units for the casserole carrier and the hand towels.*

Step 7. Arrange the units from Step 6 into 12 Nine-Patch Block A and 12 Nine-Patch Block B as shown in Fig. 2. Sew the units together to complete each square and press the seams as shown.

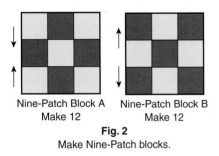

Nine-Patch Block A
Make 12

Nine-Patch Block B
Make 12

Fig. 2
Make Nine-Patch blocks.

Step 8. Sew a 6½ x 12½-inch green border strip to opposite sides of the center square and press the seams toward the borders. Sew a Nine-Patch Block A to opposite ends of each of the remaining green border strips. Press the seams toward the border strips. Sew the strips to the remaining opposite edges of the center square as shown in Fig. 3 to complete the center panel.

Step 9. Sew a 6½ x 24½-inch paisley border strip to opposite sides of the center panel. Press the seams toward the border

strips. Sew a Nine-Patch Block B to opposite ends of each of the remaining paisley border strips. Sew to the center panel and press the seams toward the border strips as shown in Fig. 4.

Step 10. Sew each 6½ x 36½-inch striped border strip to a 6½ x 36½-inch large floral print border strip. Press the seam toward the floral border strip in each unit as shown in Fig. 5. Set two border units aside for Step 11 and sew the other two to opposite sides of

the quilt center. Press the seams toward the striped borders.

Step 11. Make four checkerboard corner units as shown in Fig. 6 using the remaining Nine-Patch A and B blocks. Sew a checkerboard unit to the opposite ends of each of the two border units set aside from Step 10. Press the seams toward the border unit. Sew to opposite sides of the quilt top.

Step 12. Cut the backing fabric into two equal lengths, each

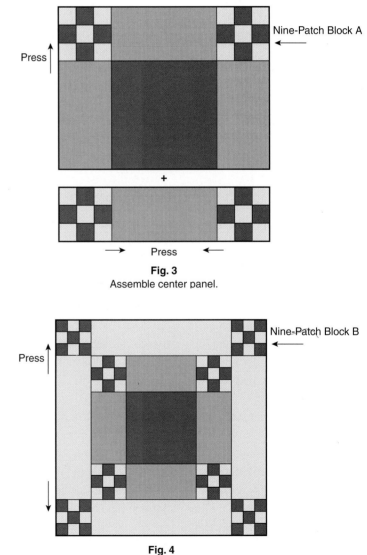

Nine-Patch Block A

Press

+

Press

Fig. 3
Assemble center panel.

Nine-Patch Block B

Press

Fig. 4
Add inner borders to center panel.

approximately 67 inches long. Split one panel lengthwise and sew the split panels to the opposite edges of the remaining panel. Press the seams toward the center panel.

Step 13. Center the batting on the wrong side of the backing and smooth out any wrinkles. Place the quilt top face up on top of the batting and pin or hand-baste the layers together. Quilt the layers together as desired. Trim the excess batting and backing even with the quilt top edges.

Step 14. Sew the binding strips together using bias seams; press the seams open. Turn under one end at a 45-degree angle and press. Trim the excess leaving a ¼-inch-wide turn-under allowance. Fold the strip in half with wrong sides together and press as shown in Fig. 7.

Step 15. Beginning in the center of one edge, pin the binding to the wrong side of the quilt. Begin stitching to the quilt a few inches from the folded end of the binding. Use a ¼-inch-wide seam allowance and miter each corner as you reach it.

Step 16. When you reach the beginning of the binding, trim the excess binding leaving enough to tuck into the folded end. Complete the stitching.

Step 17. Wrap the binding over the raw edge to the right side of the quilt, fold miters at the corners and pin in place. Machine-stitch through the folded edge of the binding for a secure application that will withstand laundering.

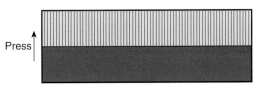

Press

Fig. 5
Make 4 border units.

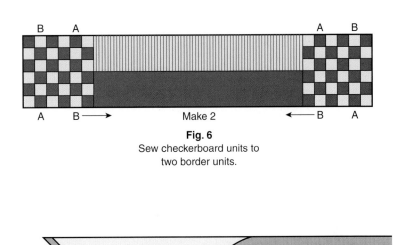

B　A　　　　　　　　　　　　　A　B

A　B →　　　Make 2　　　← B　A

Fig. 6
Sew checkerboard units to two border units.

¼" turn-under

Fig. 7
Prepare binding.

Quilt Diagram

MATERIALS

CASSEROLE CARRIER

Note: *All yardage is for 44/45-inch-wide cotton fabric.*

- ⅝ yard red-on-cream small floral print
- ⅝ yard red large floral print
- ¼ yard small red print
- ⅛ yard green tone-on-tone print
- ½ yard thin cotton batting
- 2 (¼-inch-diameter) wooden dowels, each 20 inches long
- 4 (1-inch-diameter) wooden balls with holes
- Green acrylic paint
- Wood glue
- Basic sewing supplies and tools

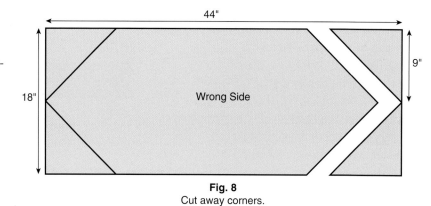

Fig. 8
Cut away corners.

INSTRUCTIONS
Casserole Carrier
Project Note: *Use ¼-inch-wide seam allowances throughout. Sew all seams with right sides together.*

Step 1. Glue wooden ball to dowel end. Paint with green acrylic paint. Allow to dry.

Step 2. From the red large floral and the red-on-cream small floral prints, cut one each 18 x 44-inch strip. Trim away the selvages. Layer the two strips with right sides together and raw edges even. Cut the short ends to a point as shown in Fig. 8. Cut the batting to match.

Step 3. Position the layered fabrics on top of the batting, smooth into place and pin the layers together. Stitch ¼ inch from the raw edges, leaving an 8-inch opening in one long edge for turning. Clip the corners and turn right side out through the opening. Press. Slipstitch the opening edges together. Topstitch ¼ inch from the finished outer edges of the panel.

Step 4. Sew leftover strip-unit sections from the table cover together to make two strips of eight squares each.

Step 5. From the green tone-on-tone print, cut two 3 x 18-inch strips. With right sides together, sew each patchwork strip to both long edges of a green strip. *Note: The green strip is wider than the patchwork strip and there will be a bubble in it when the stitching is completed.* Turn each strip right side out and press, centering the patchwork so the green shows evenly at each long edge as shown in Fig. 9.

Step 7. Position a patchwork strip at each end of the carrier on the lining side as shown in Fig. 11. Trim the ends ¼ inch beyond the carrier finished edges. Turn under and press so edges are even. Pin.

Make 8

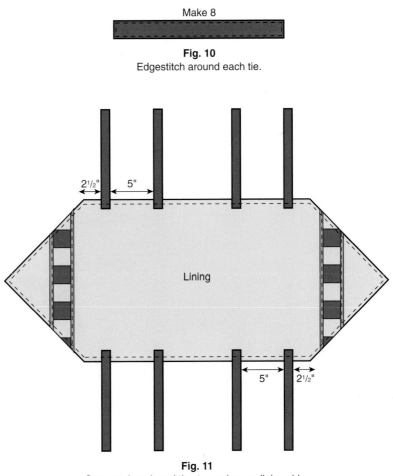

Fig. 10
Edgestitch around each tie.

2½"   5"

Lining

5"   2½"

Fig. 11
Sew patchwork and ties to carriers on lining side.

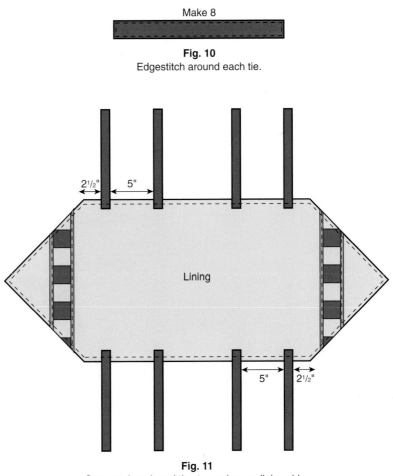

Fig. 9
Center the patchwork so green shows evenly at both long edges.

Step 6. From the small red print, cut eight 1½ x 9-inch strips for the ties. Turn under and press ¼ inch at each short end of each strip. Fold each strip in half with wrong sides together and press. Turn the raw edges in to meet the fold in each strip and press as shown in Fig. 10. Stitch close to the folded edges through all layers.

Position a narrow red tie at each edge of the carrier in the locations shown in Fig. 5 and stitch in place.

Step 8. With the outside of the carrier panel facing up, fold the pointed ends as shown in Fig. 12 and pin through all layers. Stitch in the ditch along both edges of each patchwork strip to secure the flaps and create casings for the handles.

Step 9. Position a 9 x 13-inch casserole in the carrier, tie the bows and slip a painted dowel into each casing.

MATERIALS

TOWELS

- 2 (18 x 24-inch) linen dish towels
- 2 (3 x 22-inch) strips green-on-green print
- Leftover patchwork strip-unit segments from the table cover project
- Basic sewing supplies

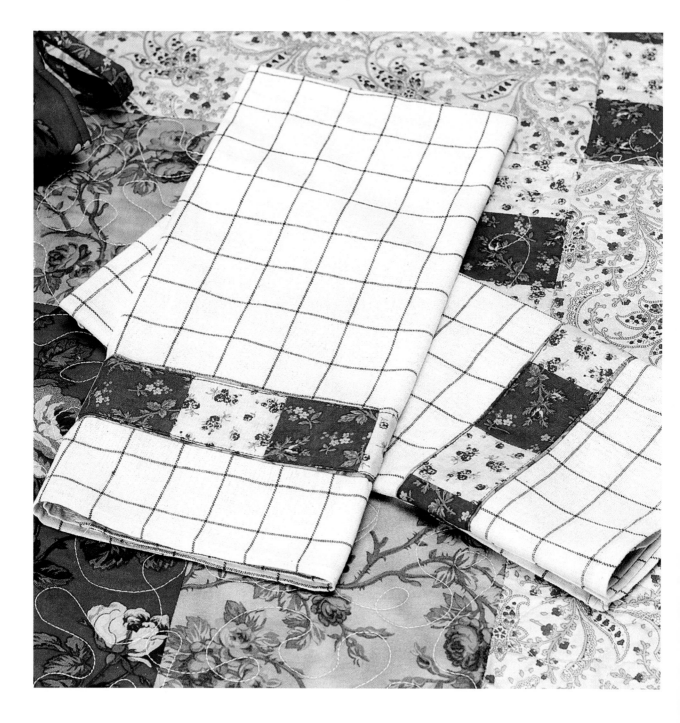

Towels

Step 1. Sew leftover patchwork from the table cover to make two strips of nine squares each.

Step 2. Center the strips along one edge of each towel 2½ inches from one end and trim excess allowing for ¼-inch turn-under

allowances at each end.

Step 3. With right sides together, sew each patchwork strip to both long edges of a 3-inch-wide green print strip as shown for the Casserole Carrier. Turn right side out and press, centering the patchwork so the green shows evenly at each long edge. Turn

under and press ¼ inch at each short edge.

Step 4. Reposition a completed strip on each towel and stitch in the ditch of the patchwork and across the ends to secure as shown for the Casserole Carrier. ∎

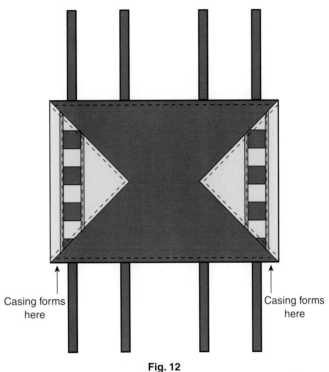

Fig. 12
Fold points to right side and
stitch in place along patchwork edges.

Casing forms here

Casing forms here

Handy Bag Holder

Gather all of your plastic bags in one tidy place by tucking them into this convenient fabric holder. A dishtowel and companion fabric print plus a bit of elastic are all it takes for this 30-minute sewing project.

DESIGN BY CAROL DACE

PROJECT SPECIFICATIONS
Skill Level: Beginner
Bag Size: 5 x 16 inches, excluding hanger

MATERIALS
- 1 cotton dishtowel at least 15½ x 21 inches
- ¼ yard 22-inch-wide coordinating fabric
- ¾ yard ¾-inch-wide elastic
- 2 (⅞-inch) decorative buttons
- All-purpose matching thread
- 1 large safety pin or a bodkin
- 2 small safety pins
- Basic sewing supplies and tools

INSTRUCTIONS
Project Note: *Prewash, dry and press the towel before cutting. Use ½-inch-wide seam allowances.*

Step 1. For the center panel of the holder, cut one rectangle 10½ x 15½ inches from the towel.

Step 2. From coordinating fabric, cut two 5½ x 15½-inch rectangles for the top and bottom panels of the holder and one 2 x 18-inch strip for the hanger.

Step 3. From the elastic, cut a 10-inch length and a 13-inch length.

Step 4. With right sides together, sew the contrasting fabric strips to the upper and lower edges of the center panel. Press the seams open and topstitch ¼ inch from each side of each seam.

Step 5. Fold the pieced panel in half lengthwise with right sides together and stitch ¼ inch from the raw edges, forming a tube. Press the seam open.

Step 6. Turn under and press ¼ inch at each end of the tube. Turn under and press an additional 1¼ inches at the top and bottom edges to make casings. Stitch close to the inner folded edge of each casing, leaving a 1-inch opening in each one to insert elastic as shown in Fig. 1. Topstitch ¼ inch from the top and bottom edges of the tube. Turn the tube right side out.

Step 7. Center the seam in the back of the tube and mark each side at the upper edge with a small safety pin.

Step 8. Using a large safety pin, thread the 13-inch length of elastic through the upper casing. Overlap the ends of the elastic ½ inch and sew together. Stitch the opening in the casing closed. Use three 10-inch length of elastic for the bottom casing.

Step 9. Fold the hanger strip in half lengthwise with wrong sides together; press. Fold the raw edges in to meet the center crease and press. Stitch close to both long edges of the hanger strip. Pin the hanger to the upper edge of the holder at the safety pins. Sew in place. Sew a button to each side of holder on top of the hanger ends.

Step 10. Tie an overhand knot in the hanger to create a loop at the top. To use, stuff plastic shopping bags into the bag through the top opening and pull out through the bottom opening as you need them. ■

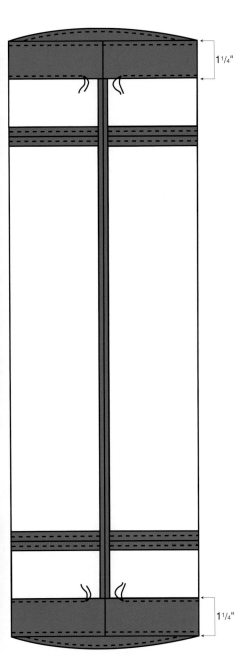

1¼"

1¼"

Fig. 1
Leave openings in casings for elastic.

Decorative Fabric Trees

Use these whimsical trees to decorate your mantel or holiday table. Get your kids involved in this project for some family fun.

DESIGN BY LEE LINDEMAN

PROJECT SPECIFICATIONS
Skill Level: Beginner
Tree Size: Approximately
6 x 12½ inches

MATERIALS

ONE TREE
- ¾ yard colored or patterned fabric
- Polyester fiberfill
- Red bead or ornament for tree topper
- Rotary cutter, mat and ruler
- Dental floss
- All-purpose thread to match fabrics
- Lightweight cardboard
- Tacky glue and/or glue gun and glue
- Hand-sewing needle with large eye
- Long doll needle
- A few small, smooth rocks for bottom weights
- Basic sewing supplies and tools

INSTRUCTIONS
Project Note: *Each tree has six sections. Use ¼-inch-wide seam allowances throughout.*

Step 1. For each tree, cut one rectangle in each of the following sizes: 1½ x 4 inches; 2½ x 6 inches; 3½ x 9 inches; 4 x 12 inches; 5 x 15 inches; and 7 x 19 inches.

Step 2. Fold each rectangle in half and stitch ¼ inch from the short ends to create a cylinder. Turn right side out. You should have 6 graduated cylinders for each tree.

Step 3. Thread the hand-sewing needle with dental floss and do a running stitch around the upper edge of one short cylinder. Draw up the floss ends to gather the top and tie to secure. Repeat at the lower edge of the cylinder, but stuff it with polyester fiberfill and then draw up the floss, leaving a 1-inch-diameter opening. Tie the floss ends to secure and then tuck a bit more fiberfill through the opening to make a plump section. Repeat with the remaining cylinders. To complete the bottom

section of each tree, wrap a few small smooth rocks in a small scrap of fabric and place in the bottom section with the polyester fiberfill to help stabilize the tree.

Step 4. With a long doll needle and dental floss, sew the sections together through the center. Add glue between the sections as you go.

Step 5. Draw and cut out a 3-inch-diameter cardboard circle for each tree. Cover circles with fabric and glue one to the bottom of each tree.

Step 6. To finish each tree, glue the red bead or ornament tree topper to the top of the tree. ∎

Snowmen Bearing Gifts

Make these three fleecy fellows with a bit of stitching and gluing to create a cheery holiday centerpiece.

DESIGN BY SHERI MCCRIMMON

PROJECT SPECIFICATIONS
Skill Level: Beginner
Centerpiece Size: Approximately 9 x 13 x 6 inches

MATERIALS
- Oval tin pail approximately 6½ x 4½ inches or a 6-inch or 7-inch round tin container
- 1⅓ cups regular uncooked rice
- 6 assorted foam snowflake cutouts
- 6 (¾-inch) white pompoms for hands
- 15 pompoms in assorted sizes (¾ –1½ inch)
- 2 (¾-inch) sparkly pompoms for hats
- ¼ yard white flannel for ground snow
- ⅓ yard white fleece for snowmen
- Assorted scraps of fleece and flannel for hats and scarves
- 1 baby sock for stocking cap
- Polyester fiberfill
- 2 (½-inch and 1-inch) gold star buttons
- 2 (⅞-inch) snowflake buttons
- 2 (1-inch) mini wrapped gift packages
- Glitter glue pen
- Powdered cosmetic blush
- Low-temperature glue gun
- 5 assorted craft mini candies
- 6 (¼-inch) black pompoms for eyes
- All-purpose threads to match fabrics
- Cotton swab

- White pipe cleaner
- Basic sewing supplies and tools

INSTRUCTIONS
Step 1. Place ¼ yard white flannel for ground snow on work surface. Color one side only with glitter glue pen, using random strokes. When dry, place in tin pail or container, arranging mounds around the outer edges, leaving the center open for snowman placement.

Step 2. From white fleece, cut three rectangles 13 x 6½ inches, 10 x 6½ inches and 8 x 6½ inches for the large, medium and small snowmen.

Step 3. Fold each snowman rectangle in half lengthwise. Sew across the end and one long side of each folded piece, leaving open at top for stuffing. Turn right side out.

Step 4. Pour ½ cup rice in each of the two taller snowmen and ⅓ cup in the smallest. Fill the remainder of each with polyester fiberfill, leaving ½ inch unfilled at the top. Sew across the top of each head ½ inch from the edge. The hats will cover the seams.

Step 5. From white fleece, cut three pieces 3½ x 7 inches for arms. Fold each in half length-wise. Sew the long edge with ½-inch seam allowance. Leave both ends open. Turn right side out.

Step 6. Turn the seam of each arm to the center back of each strip; finger-press. Use glue gun to glue a ¾-inch white pompom to each open edge of arms for hands.

Step 7. Cut the baby sock off approximately 2½ inches from the toe. Roll the cut edge of the toe portion back slightly to form a cuff. Use glue gun to glue one ¾-inch glittery pompom to toe of sock. Place on tallest snowman's head.

Step 8. For the fringed hat, cut a 6½ x 6½-inch square of colored fleece. Fold in half, right sides facing. Sew the edges opposite the fold, leaving the ends open. Turn right side out. Fold up one open end ½ inch to form band. At opposite edge cut 2½-inch strips from the top down approximately ¼ inch apart all the way around.

Step 9. With needle and thread, gather the fabric at the lower end of the cut strips. Wrap the thread around the outside two or three times and knot to secure. Place the hat on the head of the middle-size snowman. Arrange fringe as desired.

Step 10. For stocking cap, cut a 4-inch square from flannel; fold in half. Beginning at corners on either edge, cut diagonally to center fold through both thickness to make a triangle. Repeat with a second piece of flannel. Using a ¼-inch seam allowance, sew triangles together along long sides, right sides facing, leaving bottom open. Turn right side out.

Step 11. With glue gun, glue remaining sparkly pompom to pointed end of stocking cap. Turn cap opening under ½ inch and place on smallest snowman's head.

Step 12. With glue gun, glue the center of the arms to the back seam allowance of the snowmen. Place 6 inches down from the top of largest snowman, 5 inches down from top of middle-sized snowman and 4 inches down for smallest.

Step 13. With glue gun, glue ¼-inch black pompoms

approximately ¼ to ½ inch down from edges of each hat.

Step 14. From fleece or flannel scraps, cut two scarf strips 16 x 2 inches and one strip 12 x 2 inches. Cut fringe approximately 1½ inches from short edges of scarf strips and approximately ⅛ inch apart.

Step 15. Above the arms, tie the two longest scarves around the two tallest snowmen. The fringe should hang to the outside. Tie the smaller scarf to the smallest snowman.

Step 16. Glue the two mini wrapped gift packages together, then glue the outsides of the packages to the inside of the tallest snowman's hands.

Step 17. String the two snowflake and two star buttons on the white pipe cleaner. Twist at each button shank to secure in place. Twist the pipe cleaner around a pencil between the buttons to create curls. Glue the ends of the pipe cleaner to the hands of the middle-sized snowman.

Step 18. Glue the hands of the smallest snowman together in front of body. Glue the craft mini candies individually behind the hands and arms.

Step 19. Arrange snowmen in pail or tin. If using the oblong container, place the smallest snowman between the two larger snowmen. If using a round container, place the smallest snowman in front of the two larger snowmen.

Step 20. Arrange the ground snow to your satisfaction. Arrange and glue the various-sized white pompoms in front of the snowmen for snowballs.

Step 21. Place and glue various-sized foam snowflakes on the pompom snowballs.

Step 22. Use cotton swab to apply powdered cosmetic blush to cheeks of snowmen. ■

Roly-Poly Snowman Dolls

This winsome trio is sure to melt your heart on the coldest of days. It's a good project for introducing children to sewing. Help them make a batch of these dolls to decorate for the holidays or to give as gifts.

DESIGNS BY LEE LINDEMAN

PROJECT SPECIFICATIONS
Skill Level: Beginner
Large Snowman Size:
4¼ x 9 inches
Medium Snowman Size:
3½ x 7¼ inches
Small Snowman Size:
3 x 6 inches

MATERIALS
- 3 (9 x 12-inch) rectangles white felt
- Red felt or synthetic suede scraps for gloves
- 3 x 10-inch rectangle red plaid flannel for scarves
- 1¼ yards narrow lace
- 4 inches ⅛-inch-wide satin ribbon
- 2 child-size colored socks for cuff hats
- Polyester fiberfill
- Dental floss
- Large-eyed, hand-sewing needle
- All-purpose white thread
- Black tapestry thread or embroidery floss for mouths
- 6 (5mm) black round cabochons for eyes
- Small amount of orange polymer clay for noses
- ⅛-inch-thick black craft foam for buttons
- Natural branches for arms
- Small, smooth rocks (optional to weight snowmen bottoms)
- 2 inches of jute cord for curl
- Tacky glue and/or hot-glue gun
- Basic sewing supplies and tools

INSTRUCTIONS
Step 1. Cut the pieces for each snowman from the white felt. For the large snowman, cut one rectangle 2½ x 5 inches for the head, one rectangle 3½ x 9 inches for the center and one rectangle 5½ x 12 inches for the bottom. For the medium snowman, cut one rectangle 2 x 5 inches for the head, one rectangle 2½ x 7 inches for the center and one rectangle 4 x 10½ inches for the bottom. For the small snowman, cut one rectangle 2 x 5 inches for the head, one rectangle 2½ x 7 inches for the center and one rectangle 3½ x 9 inches for the bottom.

Step 2. With right sides facing, sew the two short ends of each head rectangle together using a ¼-inch-wide seam. Turn right side out.

Step 3. Using dental floss and a hand-sewing needle, do a running stitch around the upper edge of each circle for the heads. Pull the floss ends to gather tightly and knot together securely. Repeat at the lower edge of each head, filling each one with polyester fiberfill before securing the floss ends.

Step 4. Repeat Steps 2 and 3 for the center and bottom sections of each showman. If desired for added stability, wrap a smooth rock in polyester fiberfill and place in the bottom of each lower snowman circle after stuffing it with fiberfill before securing the floss ends.

Step 5. Glue the head, middle and bottom of each snowman together. From scrap felt, cut a circle for the bottom of each snowman, making it large enough to cover the bottom where the gathers are. Glue in place.

Step 6. Use black tapestry thread and a running stitch or outline stitch to make each mouth. Refer to the photo for a variety of mouth shapes.

Step 7. On each snowman, glue black cabochons in place for the "coal" buttons.

Step 8. Form noses from the orange polymer clay and bake

following the manufacturer's directions. When cool, glue the noses in place.

Step 9. Cut nine ¼-inch buttons from the black craft foam. Glue three in place on each snowman.

Step 10. From the red plaid flannel, cut two 1¼ x 10-inch strips for scarves and make fringe by removing threads for about ¼ inch at each short end of each strip. Turn under and press ⅜ inch at each long edge of each scarf and glue or zizag stitch in place. Wrap and tie a scarf around the neck of each of the two larger snowmen.

Step 11. For hats, cut off the upper 2½ inches of each sock cuff. Using dental floss, wrap and tie

the area near the cut end tightly to form a pompon. Turn up the remaining raw edge to create a cuffed brim on each hat. Position a hat on each of the two larger snowmen and glue in place.

Step 12. Make small slits in the side of each snowman's midsection. Insert branches for arms into the slits and a drop of glue to adhere them. Refer to the photo for placement.

Step 13. For the large snowman's gloves, cut two 1 x 1¼-inch pieces from red felt or synthetic suede. Fold each in half crosswise to make a ⅝ x 1-inch rectangle. Use scissors to round the two corners on one short end of each folded rectangle. Glue or edgestitch the two layers together, leaving the

bottoms open. Tuck branches inside gloves and glue in place.

Step 14. For the small snowman, cut the narrow lace trim into three lengths: 10 inches, 15 inches and 20 inches. Using dental floss and a hand-sewing needle, gather the lace to fit around the snowman at the neck, waist and bottom edge. Use the floss ends to tie the two smaller lengths around the neck and waistline. Gather and glue the longer piece to fit around the outer edge at the bottom of the snowman.

Step 15. For small snowman's topknot, untwist a 2-inch length of jute and glue in place. Tie the red satin ribbon into a bow and glue in place at the base of the topknot. ∎

Autumn Floral Duo

Make this coordinating apron and matching potholders in colors to complement your kitchen décor.

DESIGNS BY MARY AYRES

PROJECT SPECIFICATIONS
Skill Level: Beginner
Apron Size: Approximately
23½ x 30½ inches excluding ties
Pot Holder Size: Approximately
6¾ inches square

MATERIALS
- 1¾ yards 44/45-inch-wide cotton decorator or medium-weight print
- ⅜ yard 44/45-inch wide coordinating solid-colored cotton solid
- 1 (15-inch) square cotton batting
- All-purpose thread to match fabrics
- Air- or water-soluble marking pen
- Rotary cutter, mat and ruler
- Basic sewing supplies and tools

INSTRUCTIONS
Project Note: Use ¼-inch-wide seam allowances.

Apron
Step 1. From the cotton print, cut one 24 x 29-inch rectangle for the apron, one 24 x 31¼-inch rectangle for the apron lining, one 5½ x 13½-inch rectangle for the pocket and one 7½ x 13½-inch rectangle for the pocket lining. From the solid-colored cotton, cut one 2½ x 24-inch strip for the upper band, two 2 x 28-inch strips for the ties, one 2 x 24-inch strip for the neck strap and one 2½ x 13½-inch strip for the pocket upper band.

Step 2. With right sides together and raw edges even, stitch the upper band to the upper edge of the apron panel. Press the seam toward the band. Referring to Fig. 1, draw armhole cutting lines on the apron. Cut on the lines and discard the cutaway corners.

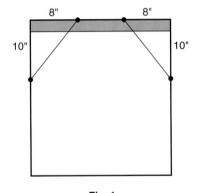

Fig. 1
Draw armhole cutting lines.

Step 3. Pin the apron to the lining panel and trim the lining to match.

Step 4. Turn under and press ¼ inch at one short end of each tie. Press. Fold each tie in half lengthwise with wrong sides together and raw edges even. Press. Turn the raw edges in to meet the fold and press. Stitch close to all turned-and-pressed edges.

Step 5. Prepare the neck strap as directed in step 4, leaving both ends unfinished.

Step 6. With right sides together and raw edges even, pin a tie to each side of the apron ¼ inch below the armhole edges as shown in Fig. 2. Position the neck strap at the upper edge of the apron ¼ inch from the armhole edges. Baste in place.

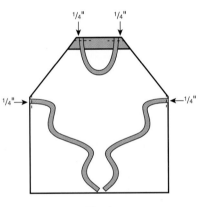

Fig. 2
Baste neck strap and ties to apron.

Step 7. With right sides together and the ties and neck strap inside, pin the apron lining to the apron. Stitch ¼ inch from all raw edges, leaving a 6-inch-long opening at the bottom for turning. Trim the corners and turn the apron right side out. Press. Slipstitch the opening closed. Topstitch ⅛ inch from the finished edges of the apron.

Step 8. With right sides together, sew the upper band to the upper edge of the pocket. Press

the seam open. With right sides together, sew the pocket to the pocket lining, leaving a 4-inch-long opening at the bottom edge for turning. Trim the corners and turn side out. Press and slipstitch the opening closed. Stitch 1/8 inch from the upper pocket edge.

Step 9. Center the pocket on the apron with the bottom edge 12 inches above the lower edge of the apron and pin in place. Topstitch 1/8 inch from the side and bottom edges. Draw a line through the pocket center to divide it into two pockets and stitch on the line.

INSTRUCTIONS
Coordinating Pot Holders

Step 1. For Potholder A (solid-color center), cut the following pieces from the print fabric: two 2½ x 3½-inch and two 2½ x 7½-inch rectangles for the front and one 7½-inch square for the back. From the solid-color fabric, cut one 3½-inch square for the front and one 2 x 5-inch strip for loop. For Potholder B (print center), cut the same pieces, reversing the fabric placement. For each pot holder, cut two 7½-inch squares of cotton batting.

Step 2. With right sides together, sew a short rectangle to each side of the center square. Press the seams open. Add the longer rectangles to the opposite sides and press the seam open.

Step 3. Baste a batting square to the wrong side of the pot holder front and back.

Step 4. Prepare the loop for each pot holder as you did the neck band for the apron (see Step 4 above), leaving both short ends unfinished. With the loop ends side by side and raw edges even, position the loop at one corner on the front of the potholder as shown in Fig. 3. Baste in place.

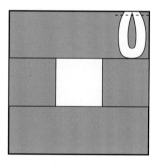

Fig. 3
Baste loop to pot holder front.

Step 5. With right sides together, sew the pot holder front to the back, leaving a 3-inch opening at one edge for turning. Trim the corners and turn right side out. Press. Slipstitch the opening closed. ∎

Beach Cover-Up & Matching Tote

You'll be ready for a fun day at the beach in this easy-to-make cover-up with its roomy matching tote!

DESIGNS BY LORI BLANKENSHIP

PROJECT SPECIFICATIONS

Skill Level: Intermediate
Beach Cover-Up Size: One size fits most (approximately 53 inches around and 30 inches long)
Tote Size: 4 x 18 x 19 inches, without handles

MATERIALS

- 2½ yards 60-inch-wide white chenille
- 1½ yards 44/45-inch-wide bright pink solid for binding, tote lining and flower appliqués
- 12 x 19-inch rectangle white muslin for pocket and tote lining
- 4 x 18-inch strip green solid for leaves
- 4 x 18-inch strip yellow solid for flowers
- 2 x 10-inch strip yellow print for flower centers
- ¾ yard paper-backed fusible web
- 1½ yards heavy-duty fusible interfacing
- 1 yard tear-away fabric stabilizer
- 3¾ x 17½-inch rectangle white craft foam or plastic canvas for tote bag bottom support
- All-purpose threads to match fabrics
- 1½- and 3-inch-diameter paper or plastic circle templates
- Rotary cutter, mat and ruler
- Basic sewing supplies and tools

INSTRUCTIONS

Project Note: *Use ½-inch seam allowance unless otherwise indicated.*

Beach Cover-Up

Step 1. From the chenille, cut one 28 x 62-inch rectangle along the fabric length so the chenille ribs run the length of the rectangle for the cover-up body. For the sleeves, cut two 14½ x 21-inch rectangles with the chenille rib running along the 14½-inch edge of the rectangle. For the pocket, cut one 10 x 12-inch rectangle with the rib along the length of the piece.

Step 2. From the bright pink fabric, cut three 3 x 44-inch strips for the cover-up binding. For the appliqués, cut one 16 x 18-inch rectangle.

Step 3. From the white muslin, cut one 7 x 10-inch rectangle for the cover-up pocket lining (cut purposely smaller than the chenille pocket piece).

Step 4. Following the manufacturer's directions, apply fusible web to the wrong side of the 16 x 18-inch pink rectangle and the 4 x 18-inch green and 2 x 10-inch yellow print strips.

Step 5. On the paper side of the fusible web, trace around the 3-inch paper circle to mark 25 pink, five green and five yellow circles. Cut out the circles. Fold the green circles in half, crease and cut in half along the crease. Using the 1½-inch paper circle, trace and cut five yellow print circles and five circles from fusible web only. Leave the paper backing on the five circles of fusible web, but remove the paper backing from all fabric pieces.

Step 6. Fold the 28 x 62-inch chenille rectangle in half to measure 28 x 31 inches. Mark the fold at the cut edges for sleeve placement. Referring to Fig.1, cut the upper layer of the panel along the center front to the fold line. Then measure and cut as shown to create the front neckline edges. Staystitch ½ inch from the front and back neckline edges.

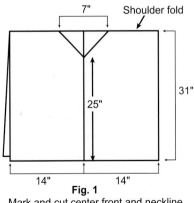

Fig. 1
Mark and cut center front and neckline through upper fabric layer only.

Step 7. Referring to the photo as a guide for the appliqué placement, arrange two rings of five pink overlapping circles to form flowers on the cover-up left front. On each ring, tuck two green half circles under the petals for leaves. Arrange the third flower and leaves to flow over the left shoulder and onto the cover-up back. Fuse all pieces in place following manufacturer's directions. Arrange the same motif with only one leaf on the 10 x 12-inch cover-up pocket, positioning the upper edge of the flower at least ¾ inch below the upper short edge of the pocket piece. Set the remaining pink and green appliqué pieces aside for the tote bag.

Step 8. Pin tear-away stabilizer to the wrong side of the fabric underneath each appliqué. Using all-purpose thread to match fabrics, satin-stitch around all cut edges. Pull the threads to the underside and tie off. Satin stitch all leaves first and then satin-stitch the flowers.

Step 9. Remove the backing paper on the four small yellow-print circles. Center each one on a solid yellow circle and fuse in place. On the wrong side of each yellow circle, center and apply a small circle of fusible web.

Step 10. Taking care not to cut into the small yellow print circle, make ½-inch-long cuts all around the outer edge of each large yellow circle to form the flower petals. Center a yellow circle on each ring of flowers and fuse in place. Satin-stitch around the outer edge of the yellow print circles. Pull

threads to the underside and tie off. Carefully remove the tear-away stabilizer.

Step 11. With right sides together, stitch the pocket lining to the upper edge of the pocket. Trim the seam to ¼ inch and press open. Pin the lining to the remaining raw edges of the pocket, allowing the pocket to roll back onto the lining as shown in Fig. 2. Stitch, leaving a 3-inch opening for turning. Clip the corners and trim the seams to ¼ inch. Turn right side out and press. Slipstitch the opening closed. Pin the pocket to right front of cover-up where desired. Topstitch in place, anchoring each upper corner with a bar tack.

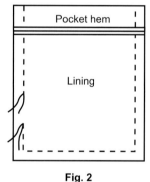

Fig. 2
Stitch lining to pocket.

Step 12. Sew two binding strips together using a bias seam and press the seam open. Cut the remaining strip into two equal lengths for the sleeves. Fold each binding strip in half lengthwise with wrong sides together and raw edges even and press.

Step 13. With right sides together and raw edges even, pin a binding strip to one long edge of each sleeve rectangle. Stitch ³/₈ inch

from the edge. Press the binding toward the seam allowance, then wrap it over and around the seam edge to the underside of the sleeve panel. From the right side, stitch in the ditch of the seam to attach the binding as shown in Fig. 3. Fold the sleeve in half to find the shoulder placement and mark at the upper raw edge.

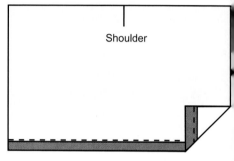

Fig. 3
Stitch in the ditch of binding seam from right side.

Step 14. With right sides together, raw edges even and shoulder marks matching, pin a sleeve to each side edge of the cover-up. Stitch ½ inch from the raw edges and press the seam toward the sleeve. Zigzag or serge the seam allowances together. With right sides together, stitch the sleeve underarm. Continue to the side seams, rounding the seam across the corner. End the side-seam stitching 4 inches above the lower edge on each side to allow for side slits. Clip the underarm curve and press the seams open and continue along the slit to the lower edge. Zigzag or serge-finish the seam edges individually. To finish the slits, topstitch ¼ inch from the pressed edges.

Step 15. Bind the cover-up front and back neckline edges as directed for the sleeves.

Step 16. Serge or zigzag the lower raw edges of the cover-up. Turn under and press a 1-inch-wide hem. Beginning and ending at the front-edge binding, topstitch the hem in place ¼ inch from the finished hem edge. Hand sew the hem sections where the binding is.

INSTRUCTIONS
Tote Bag

Step 1. From the chenille, cut one 19 x 42-inch rectangle for the tote body, two 5 x 19-inch rectangles for the tote side panels and two 5 x 31-inch strips for the tote straps. Make sure the chenille rib runs the length of all pieces.

Step 2. From the bright pink fabric cut one 19 x 42-inch rectangle. Cut two 5 x 19-inch rectangles for the tote lining, and two 14-inch squares for the pockets. From the muslin, cut one 5 x 19-inch rectangle for the pocket for the tote bottom support.

Step 3. From the fusible interfacing, cut one 18 x 41-inch rectangle and two 4 x 18-inch rectangles.

Step 4. With right sides together, fold the 19 x 42-inch tote panel in half crosswise and mark the fold at each edge. Unfold and place face down on a flat surface. Fold the 5 x 19-inch muslin strip in half lengthwise and mark the fold at each short edge. Open the rectangle and center it on the wrong side of the tote with the marks matching. Stitch ¼ inch from two long edges and one short edge. Slide the piece of white craft foam into the pocket and stitch the end closed.

Step 5. Adjust the sewing machine for 18-20 stitches per inch. Staystitch ½ inch from the tote raw edges as shown in Fig. 4. Make the appliqué for the tote bag following Steps 7-10 in the directions for the cover-up. Center the flower appliqué on the tote panel and sew in place as shown in Fig. 4.

Step 6. With right sides together, pin a side panel to the tote beginning at one upper edge. Pin to within a few inches of the bottom corner and then clip the tote panel to the staystitching as needed to turn the corner. Continue pinning the side panel to the tote, clipping as needed to turn the second corner. Stitch from the tote side, pivoting at the corners as shown in Fig. 5. Repeat with the remaining tote panel. Turn the tote right side out and set aside.

Step 7. Fold each long strip for the straps in half lengthwise with right sides together. Stitch ¼ inch from the long raw edges. Turn right side out and press, centering the seam on the underside of each strap. Do a double row of topstitching through the center of each strap, spacing the rows ¼ inch apart. With right sides together, pin the strap ends to the upper edges of the tote front and back, placing the outer edges of the straps 4 inches in from the side seam edges. Stitch in place ³/₈ inch from the raw edges. Machine baste ½ inch from the upper edge of the tote bag, leaving long thread tails.

Step 8. Turn under and press ½ inch along the side and bottom edges of each 14-inch-square lining pocket. Make a narrow double hem in the remaining upper edge of each pocket.

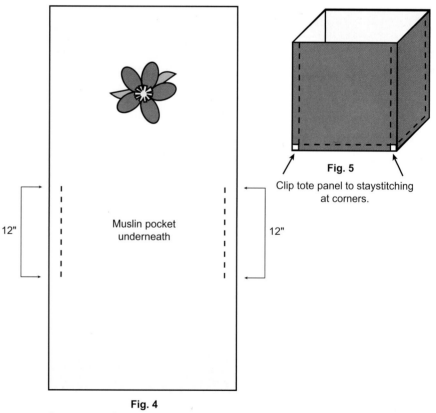

Fig. 5
Clip tote panel to staystitching at corners.

12" · · · · Muslin pocket underneath · · · · 12"

Fig. 4
Staystitch ½" from long edges of tote panel.

Step 9. Following manufacturer's directions, fuse the interfacing pieces to the wrong side of the tote lining pieces. Staystitch the lining panel as shown for the tote in Fig. 4. Draw a line straight across the interfacing 18½ inches from one short edge. Draw a second line 4 inches below the first. Fold and crease the lining pieces along the marked lines.

Step 10. Unfold the lining. Position a pocket with the lower edge 1 inch above one of the folds and the hemmed edge toward the upper raw edge of the lining panel. Center it from side to side and pin in place. Edgestitch in place along the side and bottom edges. Position the remaining pocket above the other fold and stitch in place.

Step 11. Sew the side panels to the lining as directed in Step 7. Insert the tote into the lining with right sides together and the straps tucked inside between the tote and lining. Pin the raw edges together at the seamlines and then pin the remaining edges together, drawing up the bobbin thread in the basting to ease the tote to the lining as needed. (The chenille may have stretched during handling.) Stitch ½ inch from the upper edges, leaving a 6-inch opening for turning. Turn the tote right side out and press the upper edge. Slipstitch the opening closed. Topstitch ¼ inch from the upper edge of the finished tote. ■

Free-as-a-Breeze Sundress

It takes a few simple measurements to stitch up this simple little sundress in rayon challis or other soft fabric. Make it in terrycloth for an oh-so-comfy beach cover-up.

DESIGN BY BY CAROL ZENTGRAF

PROJECT SPECIFICATIONS
Skill Level: Confident beginner
Sundress Size: Any size

MATERIALS
Materials listed are for a Misses Medium with a finished length of 32 inches. Adjust yardage as needed for your size after determining the cutting dimensions as directed in Steps 1–7.

- 1⅝ yards 54-inch-wide light- to medium-weight fabric such as rayon challis*
- 1 yard ¾-inch-wide elastic for upper edge
- Water- or air-soluble marking pen
- All-purpose thread to match fabric
- Pattern tracing cloth or paper with a 1-inch grid
- Basic sewing supplies and tools

***Note**: For small sizes (hip measurement less than 36 inches), you can purchase 44/45-inch-wide fabric.*

INSTRUCTIONS
Project Note: *Use ½-inch-wide seam allowances unless otherwise noted, and stitch*
all seams with right sides together. Directions are given for making full-size pattern pieces, customized to your body measurements. If you feel comfortable doing so, you can draw the shapes directly on the fabric rather than making the pattern first.*

Step 1. Measure and make note of your bustline and full hip measurements.

Step 2. Standing in front of a full-length mirror, have a sewing friend measure the length from the desired location of the dress upper edge to your waistline and to the desired finished length. Make note of both measurements. In addition, measure and note the distance from your waistline to the fullest part of your hipline.

Step 3. On the gridded paper or pattern tracing cloth, draw a rectangle that is the desired length from the finished upper edge to the hemline and 5 inches wider than ¼ of your full hip measurement. For example, the width
for a full-hip measurement of 36 inches would be 11½ inches (¼ x 36 = 9 + 2½ = 11½).

Step 4. At the upper edge of the box, make a mark that is ¼ of your full bust measurement plus 1 inch. Draw a slightly curved line for the dress upper edge, tapering it so it is 1 inch lower at the side seam.

Step 5. Mark the waistline location, drawing it ½ inch lower than the distance from the upper edge to your waistline as determined in Step 2.

Step 6. Measure down and mark the full hip location. Using a ruler, connect the lower edge of the box with a straight line. From the hip to the waistline, taper in slightly, then taper from the waist to the upper edge as shown in Fig. 1.

Step 7. At the upper edge, add ½ inch for the seam allowance. At the lower edge, add 1½ inches for the hem allowance. For the dress back, cut a matching pattern piece, making the upper edge straight across from the side seam edge to the center front and adding ½ inch for the upper-edge seam allowance. On each pattern piece, measure 8 inches down from the underarm and draw a bodice lining cutting line. Cut out the front and back pattern pieces.

Step 8. Fold the fabric lengthwise with selvages meeting in the center. Position the front and back pattern pieces on the folds and pin in place as shown in Fig. 2; cut out. From the remaining fabric, cut front and back lining pieces using

the cutting lines marked in Step 7. For the optional straps, cut two 3 x 12-inch strips. For the tie belt, cut two 4 x 36-inch strips.

Step 9. Sew the dress front and back together at the side seams, leaving the lower 18 inches of each seam unstitched for slits. Serge-finish the raw edges of the seam allowances and press open, continuing to the hem edge in the slit area. Topstitch the slit ¼ inch from the turned edge as shown in Fig. 3.

Step 10. With right sides facing, fold each strap in half lengthwise and stitch ½ inch from the raw edges. Centering the seam, stitch across one short end as shown in Fig. 4. Turn right side out and press, centering the seam on the underside of each strap. Set aside.

Step 11. Sew the front and back lining pieces together at the side seams and press the seams open. Finish the lower edge with serging or zigzagging, or turn under and stitch ¼ inch to clean-finish.

Step 12. With right sides facing, stitch the lining to the upper edge of the dress. Trim the seam to ¼ inch and

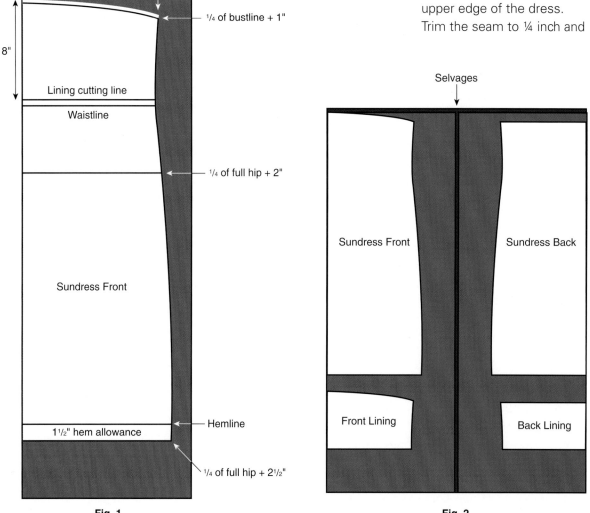

Fig. 1
Draft front pattern.

Fig. 2
Pin patterns to folded fabric.

underststitch. Turn the lining to the inside and press. Topstitch ¼ inch from the upper edge.

Step 13. Beginning at one side seam and leaving a 2-inch opening, topstitch 1 inch below the first topstitching to create the casing.

Step 14. To determine the cut length for the elastic, wrap it snugly around your chest (upper bustline) and add 1 inch to this measurement.

Step 15. Insert the elastic in the casing through the opening. Pin the ends together and try on the dress. Adjust the elastic to fit, then overlap and stitch the ends

together in an X. Complete the casing stitching.

Step 16. For the optional straps, try the dress on and position the finished ends of the straps ½ inch below the front edge of the sundress, placing them an equal distance from center front. Pin in place securely. Have someone adjust the straps in back to the desired length. Remove the dress. Topstitch the straps in place in front on top of the original topstitching, stitching three times for added security. In back, cut away any excess strap length, leaving ¼ inch to turn under and edgestitch. Topstitch the straps to the dress back as for the front.

Step 17. Sew the two tie belt strips together at the short ends, using a ¼-inch-wide seam. Press the seam open. Fold the strip in half lengthwise with right sides together and stitch ¼ inch from the raw edges, leaving an opening in the center for turning. Turn right side out and press. Slipstitch the opening closed. Tie an overhand knot at each end of the finished belt.

Step 18. Try on the finished dress and tie the belt around your waist. Mark the desired hemline. A 1½-inch-wide hem was allowed, but you may make it narrower as you wish. Hem as desired. ■

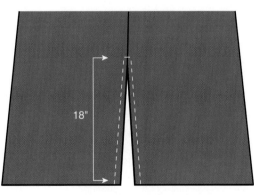

Fig. 3
Topstitch the slit.

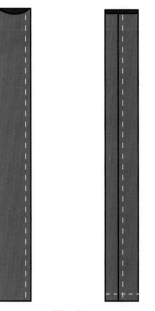

Fig. 4
Stitch. Center the seam and stitch across one end.

Side-Slit Skirt & Scarf

A lightweight border print is ideal for this breezy skirt with a side slit and slightly gathered waist. Make a matching fringed scarf from the fabric left after cutting the skirt.

DESIGNS BY CAROL ZENTGRAF

PROJECT SPECIFICATIONS

Skill Level: Beginner
Skirt Size: Misses size 8
Scarf Size: Approximately 10½ x 60 inches excluding fringe

MATERIALS

Note: *Materials listed are for a Misses size 8 with a finished length of 35½ inches. For each size larger, add 3 inches to the yardage required for a size 8.*

- 1¼ yards 54/60-inch-wide lightweight border print
- ⅔ yard 3-inch-long fringe
- 1 yard 1-inch-wide elastic
- All-purpose thread to match fabrics
- 1½-inch diameter decorative button
- Air- or water-soluble marking pen
- Large safety pin or bodkin
- Sewing machine twin needle (optional)
- Basic sewing supplies and tools

INSTRUCTIONS

Side-Slit Skirt

Project Note: *Use the following measurements as a size guide: size 8, hips 37 inches; size 10, hips 38 inches; size 12, hips 39½ inches; size 14, hips 41½ inches. Cutting instructions are for a size 8. Add ½ inch to the width of the* skirt front and back pattern pieces for each size larger (that's 1 inch total to each piece). Decrease the width by the same amount for each size smaller. Adjust the waistband length in the same manner. Use ½-inch-wide seam allowances.

Step 1. Straighten the cut edges of the fabric by pulling a thread and cutting along the pull. Fold the skirt fabric as shown in Fig. 1 with selvages aligned and cut edges meeting at the center.

Step 2. Mark the skirt and waistband shapes as shown in Fig. 2 with the border design at the lower, straight edge of the skirt pieces. (Adjust the length of the skirt panels if desired.) Cut out the pieces. The cut waistband strips should each measure 3½ x 19 inches.

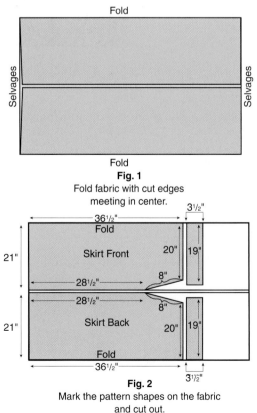

Fold

Selvages · Selvages

Fold

Fig. 1
Fold fabric with cut edges meeting in center.

36½"
3½"
Fold
21"
Skirt Front
20"
19"
28½"
8"
28½"
8"
21"
Skirt Back
20"
19"
Fold
36½"
3½"

Fig. 2
Mark the pattern shapes on the fabric and cut out.

Step 3. With right sides together, pin the skirt front to the back along both side seams, leaving the lower 16½ inches unpinned on the left side and taking care to match the border print. Stitch the side seams as shown in Fig. 3 and press them open, continuing along the slit opening edges. Turn the raw edge of the slit allowance in to the pressed edge to create a narrow hem around the slit and topstitch in place. Turn the skirt right side out.

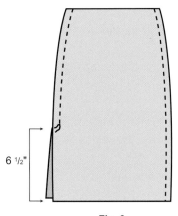

6 ½"

Fig. 3
Stitch seams, leaving slit
opening on left side.

Step 4. With right sides together, sew the short ends of the waistband pieces together to create a circle. Machine baste ½ inch from one long edge. Using the basting as a guide, turn under and press the seam allowance. Remove the basting.

Step 5. With right sides together and raw edges even, stitch the waistband to the skirt upper edge. Press the band toward the seam allowance. Turn the waistband to the inside with the folded edge ⅛ inch beyond the waistline stitching and pin in place. Topstitch in place, leaving a 2-inch-long opening to insert the elastic.

Step 6. Wrap the elastic around your waist and cut a comfortable length, allowing an extra inch for overlapping. Insert the elastic through the waistband opening using a large safety pin or bodkin. Overlap the ends and stitch securely. Topstitch the waistband opening closed.

Step 7. To hem the skirt, turn under and press a ½ inch at the lower edge of the skirt. The selvage creates a finished edge. Topstitch and edgestitch or use a twin needle to stitch the hem in place.

Step 8. Sew a decorative button above the slit.

INSTRUCTIONS
Scarf

Step 1. Cut two 11 x 59-inch panels from the remaining fabric.

Step 2. With right sides together and raw edges even, sew the two panels together along both long edges and one short end. Turn right side out and press. Turn under and press ½ inch at the open end and slipstitch or topstitch the layers together.

Step 3. Cut two 11-inch lengths of fringe and turn under ½ inch on each end to prevent raveling. Pin the fringe heading to the scarf ends and topstitch in place. ∎

Sassy Classy Lady

Make this set of wardrobe pieces in no time at all. The 54-inch heavy cotton or linen fabric is made oh so pretty by adding button tabs and a contrasting lining.

DESIGNS BY PEARL LOUISE KRUSH

PROJECT SPECIFICATIONS

Skill Level: Beginner
Vest Size: Medium size 10
Skirt Size: Medium size 10
Purse Size: 11 x 8 x 3 inches, excluding handle

MATERIALS

Note: *If increasing skirt size, purchase an additional yard of fabric.*

- 3 yards 54-inch-wide heavy cotton or linen fabric for vest, skirt and purse
- ¾ yard 54-inch-wide contrasting cotton fabric for vest lining
- 2 (½-inch) flat buttons for skirt
- 12 (½-inch) shank buttons for vest
- 2 (¾-inch) shank buttons for vest
- 2 (½-inch) shank buttons for purse
- 4 (¾-inch) shank buttons for purse
- 1 (9-inch) paper plate
- Basic sewing supplies and tools

INSTRUCTIONS

Project Note: *Read all instructions before beginning. To make vest larger or smaller, cut the tabs longer or shorter accordingly. To make the vest neck-hole template, cut a 9-inch paper plate in fourths. Keep one of the fourths as your template. Use a ¼-inch seam allowance.*

Vest

Step 1. For the vest, cut one rectangle 24 x 44 inches, and one strip 2¼ x 54 inches for button tabs from heavy cotton or linen fabric. For the vest lining, cut one rectangle 24 x 44 inches from the contrasting cotton lining fabric.

Step 2. Place vest and lining fabrics right sides together. Fold in half widthwise, folding top down to bottom so that fold is at the top. The top fold will be your shoulder line. Next, fold in half lengthwise, folding the left side over to the right so that fold is on the left. The fabric will now measure 12 inches across by 22 inches down.

Step 3. Place the neck-hole template in the upper left-hand corner as shown in Fig. 1, matching the straight sides of the template to the side and top folds. Pin template and trace around curved side. Cut along traced line to make neck-hole opening.

Step 4. Unfold the fabric and determine which side is the front. For the center-front opening, mark and cut from front neck center down to the center

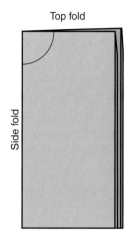

Fig. 1
Trace around neckline template; cut on line.

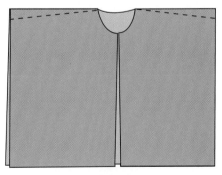

Fig. 2
Taper shoulder seams to fit your shoulder slope.

bottom (Fig. 2). If desired, you may also cut open the shoulder fold to allow for a better fit, but this is not necessary.

Step 5. If shoulder fold was cut, sew vest fronts to back at shoulders, right sides together. Press seams open. Repeat for lining.

Step 6. Place the vest and lining right sides together. Beginning at the bottom, sew together up one front side, around neck hole and down remaining front side. Clip to sewn line in curves. Sew vest and lining together at sides (Fig. 3). Turn right sides out and press. For each front bottom hem, turn under ¼ inch and press. Turn under an additional ½ inch, press and top-stitch. Repeat for back hem.

Step 7. For tabs, fold tab strip in half lengthwise, right sides together. Sew together down long side, leaving ends open. Measuring down the length of the strip, left to right, mark and cut six segments 4 inches long (adjust length if needed) and one 6-inch-long segment as shown in Fig. 4.

Note: There will be extra length left over. Turn each segment right side out. Center seam in back and turn in ¼ inch on each end and press. Topstitch across ends.

Step 8. For center neck tab, sew buttonholes in each end of the 6-inch tab. For button placement, measure down 1¾ inches from neckline and in 1¼ inches from the center-front-opening sides. Mark placement and sew on ¾-inch shank buttons.

Step 9. For side tab placement, measure 11 inches down from top of the shoulder seam and mark. From that, measure down 3 inches and mark for second tab. From that, measure down 3 inches and mark for last tab. Repeat to mark other vest sides. Side tabs may be attached by sewing buttonholes in each tab end and sewing the ½-inch shank buttons onto the vest, or by sewing the buttons and tabs on at the same time.

Step 10. At top of each shoulder, fold contrasting lining up and over the shoulder 1¾ inches. Tack in place. Angle the fold down to ½-inch wide 1 inch above first tab. Tack in place.

INSTRUCTIONS
Skirt
Project Note: To determine the waistband length for a size different from the one used, measure your waist and add 17 inches. If enlarging the skirt, add an 8 x 36-

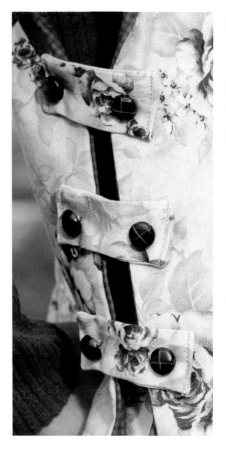

inch panel for each size increase. Use ¼-inch seam allowance.

Step 1. From the heavy cotton or linen fabric, cut one strip 2 x 45 inches for the waistband, one rectangle 36 x 54 inches for the skirt, and any panels if needed.

Step 2. Press skirt sides under ¾ inch. (If adding panels, sew to sides first and press seams open.) Fold raw edges under ¼ inch. Press and topstitch close to edge. For skirt hem, press under ½ inch. Fold under ½ inch again and top-stitch in place.

Step 3. To mark darts, fold skirt

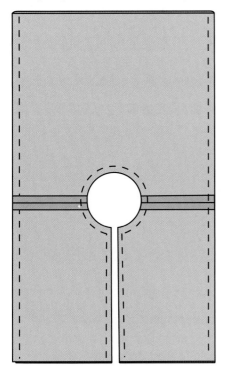

Fig. 3
Stitch vest to lining.

4"	4"	4"	4"	4"	4"	6"	

Fig. 4
Cut tabs from fabric tube; for larger sizes, cut longer side tabs and adjust when fitting vest.

in half lengthwise. Mark fold with pin. Fold in half lengthwise again and mark each fold with pins. Fold in half lengthwise one more time and mark each fold with pins. **Note:** *Folded skirt will now measure approximately 6½ x 53 inches.* This will give you markings for seven darts.

Step 4. Mark and sew a ½-inch-wide by 4-inch-long dart at each pin (Fig. 5). Place the skirt top on the waistband with waistband ends extending ¾ inch beyond skirt sides. If needed, fit skirt to waistband by adding additional darts either side of the center dart. Pin the waistband and skirt right sides together and sew. Press seam allowance toward waistband. Press waistband ends under ¼ inch. Fold top edge of waistband under ¼ inch and press. Fold waistband in half to inside of skirt and pin. Topstitch in place.

Step 5. Sew a buttonhole at each end of waistband.

Step 6. Wrap the skirt around your waist and mark for button placement on the inside and outside where the skirt folds over. Sew ½-inch flat buttons in place to finish.

INSTRUCTIONS
Purse
Step 1. From the heavy cotton or linen fabric, cut four rectangles 8½ x 11½ inches for purse front, back and lining, and four rectangles 4½ x 11½ inches for pockets and lining. Cut two rectangles 3½ x 29 inches for purse sides/bottom and lining, and one strip 4 x 54 inches for purse strap. From scraps, cut two rectangles 2 x 6 inches for purse tab.

Step 2. Place a pocket and pocket lining right sides together. Sew together at top. Turn right sides out. Press. Topstitch across top ¼ inch from edge. Repeat with remaining pocket.

Step 3. Place a pocket on the right side of purse front, matching bottom edges. Pin. Sew together from the top center of the pocket down to the bottom center to divide into two pockets. Repeat to sew other pocket to purse back.

Step 4. Pin purse sides/bottom strip to purse front sides and bottom, right sides together. Trim sides/bottom piece to fit. Sew. Pin other side of strip to purse back sides and bottom, right sides together. Sew. Repeat with purse lining pieces.

Step 5. Turn purse right sides out. Fold top edge down ½ inch toward inside. Press. Repeat with lining. Turn lining wrong side out and insert into purse, matching top edges. Pin and set aside.

Step 6. Fold purse strap in half lengthwise, right sides together. Sew together along length, leaving ends open. Turn right side out. Center seam in back and press. Insert 2 inches of strap end at each side, between purse and lining. Pin in place.

Step 7. Topstitch around the purse top ¼ inch from top edge (Fig. 6). Topstitch again ¼ inch below the first topstitching.

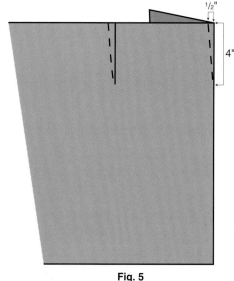

Fig. 5
Fold skirt at pins; mark and stitch darts.

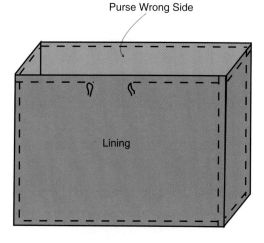

Fig. 6
Stitch lining to purse, leaving 5" opening for turning.

Step 8. Place the two purse tab pieces right sides together. Sew long sides together. Turn right side out and turn in ¼ inch on ends. Press. Topstitch close to end edges. Make a buttonhole on each end. Sew a ¾-inch shank button to center top front and one to the center top back of purse.

Step 9. Sew two (½-inch) shank buttons on the back pockets, 1 inch below top edge of pockets. Repeat with two (¼-inch) shank buttons on front pockets, 1 inch below top edge of pockets. ■

Sophisticate in Plaid

These easy-fitting wardrobe coordinates are the perfect choice for lunch, shopping or an important business appointment. The matching bag is the perfect finishing touch. Substitute fabrics in your favorite colors to complement your style.

DESIGNS BY LORI BLANKENSHIP

PROJECT SPECIFICATIONS
Skill Level: Intermediate
Dress Size: Any size
Jacket Size: Any size
Shoulder Bag Size: 11¾ x 13¾ inches, excluding strap

MATERIALS
- 2½ yards 44/45-inch-wide light- to medium-weight fabric for dress and shoulder bag
- 2½ yards 44/45-inch-wide coordinating lining fabric for dress and shoulder bag
- 1½ yards 44/45-inch-wide coordinating plaid fabric for jacket
- ⅛ yard medium-weight, woven or nonwoven fusible interfacing for jacket button tabs
- 1⅓ yards 1-inch-wide coordinating single-fold bias tape for jacket
- ⅔ yard ½-inch-wide coordinating single-fold bias tape for jacket
- 13 x 29-inch piece medium- to heavyweight fusible interfacing for backing for shoulder bag
- 2 yards coordinating twisted cord for shoulder bag handle
- All-purpose matching thread
- 5 (25mm) buttons
- 4 (19mm) buttons
- 1 (⅝-inch-diameter) hook-and-loop dot closure

- Rotary cutter, mat and ruler
- Chalk wheel
- Paper and pencil
- 8-inch paper circle
- Liquid seam sealant
- Basic sewing supplies and tools

INSTRUCTIONS
Project Note: *Seam allowances vary. Follow the directions with each step.*

Dress
Step 1. To make the armhole template, draw a rectangle measuring 2½ x 8 inches. Referring to Fig. 1, place your pencil on the lower left-hand corner and draw a line at a 45-degree angle out from the corner, measuring 1½ inches. Next measure 2¼ inches up each side from the lower left-hand corner and mark. Connect the side markings with the end of the corner line to form a curve, again referring to Fig. 1. Cut away the corner along the curve and discard. (For larger sizes, increase the width of the template to enlarge the armhole as needed.)

Step 2. To make the dress neckline template, fold the 8-inch paper

circle in half and then in half again to locate the center. Measure 1 inch up from the center and mark as shown in Fig. 2.

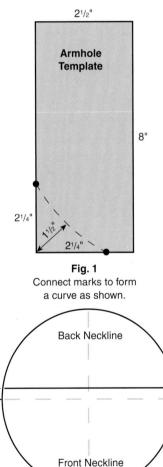

Fig. 1
Connect marks to form a curve as shown.

Fig. 2
Draw line across circle 1" above center.

Step 3. To determine how wide to cut the rectangle for the dress front and back, measure the fullest part of your hips and add 4½ inches for ease and seam allowances. Divide the result by 2. For example, if your hips measure 36 inches, the measurement would be 40½ inches divided by 2, or 20¼ inches.

Step 4. Straighten both cut ends of the fabric. Fold the fabric in half crosswise with selvages and cut edges even. The fold line is the shoulder line and the piece should measure approximately 45 inches square. Using the measurement determined in Step 3, trim each piece of fabric to the correct width. Repeat with the lining fabric. Set aside the fabric cutaways to use later.

Step 5. Referring to Fig. 3, position the armhole template at the outer edges in the upper corner of the folded dress-fabric rectangle with the upper edge of the template along the fold line. Pin in place. Cut out around the template. Reverse the template and cut the armhole at the opposite edge of the folded dress fabric. Repeat with the folded lining fabric. Locate the center of the folded edge and mark.

Step 6. Unfold the dress and lining pieces and place them right sides together with raw edges even. Pin together around the armhole edges. Fold in half crosswise and crease lightly to mark the center, then unfold and refold crosswise. Crease lightly to mark the center.

Step 7. As shown in Fig. 4, pin the neckline template in place on the fabric, matching the line you drew with the shoulder crease. Trace around the outer edge of the template with the chalk wheel. Remove the template and stitch on the chalk line. **Note:** *The deeper side of the circle is the front neckline.* Cut out the center of the circle leaving a ¼-inch-wide seam allowance inside the stitching line. Clip the curves every ¼ inch. Turn the dress right side out and press, making sure the lining rolls to the underside so it doesn't peek out at the neckline edge. Understitch the lining to the seam allowance if desired. Topstitch the lining in place ¼ inch from the finished edge.

Step 8. Keeping the lining free of the dress, pin the dress seams with right sides together. Leave the lower 12 inches of the left side seam in the dress unpinned to allow for a walking slit. Stitch the

pinned side seams ⅝ inch from the raw edges and press open. To finish the slit, turn under and press the seam allowance and then turn the raw edge in to the fold and press. Topstitch in place. Repeat with the lining, leaving the walking slit area open in the *right* side seam since the right side of the lining will be against you when you wear the dress.

Step 9. *With wrong sides together* and raw edges even, pin the dress to the lining around the

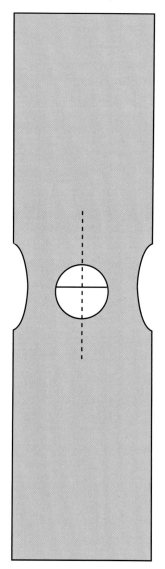

Fig. 4
Position template on layered fabrics
with line at shoulder crease
and centers matching.

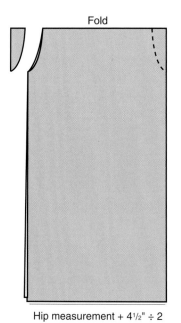

Hip measurement + 4½" ÷ 2
Fig. 3
Position template at upper corners of
folded dress fabric and cut away
excess to shape armholes.

armholes. Stitch ⅝ inch from the raw edges. Carefully turn under and press the seam allowance along the stitching. Turn under the raw edge to meet the pressed edge and press. Pin in place and then topstitch through all layers along the inner folded edge to finish each armhole.

Step 10. For the dress pockets, cut two rectangles each 5 x 6½ inches from the dress fabric cutaways and two from the lining cutaways from Step 4. From the jacket fabric, cut two rectangles 3½ x 5 inches for the dress pocket flaps and two rectangles 2 x 3 inches for the dress pocket tabs. Cut one rectangle 4½ x 6 inches for the neckline flap and one rectangle 2½ x 5 inches for the tab.

Step 11. With right sides together and raw edges even, pin each pocket to a pocket lining. Stitch ½ inch from the raw edges, leaving a 3-inch opening in one short edge for turning. Clip the corners and trim the seams to ¼ inch. Turn right side out and press, rolling the lining to the underside along the pocket edges so it doesn't show on the right side. Slipstitch the opening closed.

Step 12. Fold each pocket flap in half with right sides together, forming a 2½ x 3½-inch rectangle. Stitch ½ inch from the short edges. Trim the seams to ¼ inch and clip the corners. Turn right side out and press. Machine baste ½ inch from the raw edges.

Step 13. Fold each tab in half to make a 1½ x 2-inch rectangle. Stitch ¼ inch from the long raw edges and one short edge. Clip the corner, turn right side out and press. Machine baste ½ inch from the raw edges.

Step 14. Referring to Fig. 5, position a tab on each pocket flap and stitch in place along the basting. Stitch again ¼ inch from the first stitching and trim seam allowance close to second row of stitching. Flip the tab down over the raw edges and press. Referring to Fig. 6, center a tabbed flap face down on each pocket and stitch to the pocket along the machine basting; stitch and trim as described above for the tab. Remove the basting. Turn the flap down over the raw edges and press. Sew a 19mm button in place through all layers to hold the flap in place.

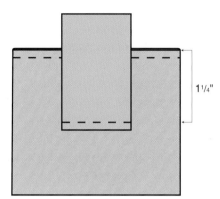

Fig. 5
Stitch tab to flap along basting.

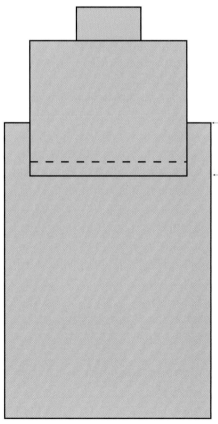

Fig. 6
Stitch tabbed flap to pocket right side.

Step 15. Try on the dress and position the pockets as desired. Pin in place and remove the dress. Topstitch in place ¼ inch from the finished edges. Make a machine bar tack at each upper corner to reinforce.

Step 16. For the neckline tabbed flap, fold the 4½ x 6-inch rectangle in half with right sides together to make a 3 x 4½-inch rectangle. Stitch ½ inch from the short edges. Trim the seams to ¼ inch, clip the corners, turn right side out and press. Machine baste ½ inch from the raw edges. Fold the tab in half with right sides together to make a 2½-inch square. Stitch ½ inch from two adjacent edges. Trim the seams to ¼ inch, clip the corner, turn right side out and press. Machine baste ½ inch from the raw edge. Center and stitch the tab to the flap as shown for the dress pocket flap. Center the tabbed flap face down with the raw edge 1 inch below the finished neckline edge. Stitch in place along the basting. Stitch a second time and trim close to the stitching. Turn the flap down over the raw edges and press. Center a 25mm button on the tab and sew in place through all layers.

Step 17. To hem the dress, turn under and press ½ inch. Turn again, press and topstitch. To hem the lining slightly shorter than the dress so it doesn't show, turn under and press ¾ inch. Turn under again, press and topstitch.

INSTRUCTIONS
Jacket
Step 1. Straighten the cut edges of the jacket fabric by cutting along a pulled thread. Fold the straight-ened fabric in half crosswise with the cut edges and selvages even. *Note: Add 2 inches to the width* determined in Step 3 for the dress and trim the folded jacket fabric panel to this width. For example, if you cut your dress panels 20¼-inch wide, you will cut the jacket panels 22¼-inch wide. Set the remaining fabric aside for the sleeves and pocket flaps.

Step 2. With the plaid fabric still folded in half, fold it in half length-wise and lightly crease to locate the center. Unfold and mark the outer cut edges at the fold for the shoulder placement.

Step 3. From the jacket fabric set aside in Step 2, cut two 18 x 20-inch rectangles for the sleeves. Mark the center of one long edge of each sleeve rectangle.

Step 4. With right sides together and the mark on the sleeve at the shoulder mark on the jacket panel, pin and stitch the sleeve rectangles to the jacket ⅝ inch from the raw edges. Use the seam finish of your choice as appropriate for the chosen fabric. Press the seam toward the sleeve.

Step 5. With right sides together, pin the underarm and sides together in continuous seams. Finish the seams as desired and press.

Step 6. Turn under and press ½ inch at the lower edge of each sleeve. Turn again, press and topstitch close to the inner folded edge.

Step 7. For the neckline template, draw and cut out a 6-inch paper circle. Fold in fourths to find and mark the center. Cut in half along the center fold.

Step 8. Arrange the jacket with sleeves on a large flat surface with

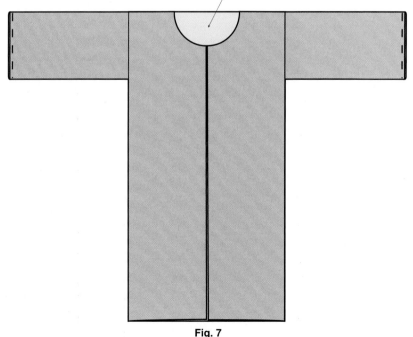

Neckline Template

Fig. 7
Slash jacket front along center front crease.

bottom raw edges even. Position the half-circle template at the fold with the centers matching as shown in Fig. 7. Pin in place and chalk mark around the half-circle. Cut along the traced line, cutting through both layers of the jacket. Cut from the lower front edge to the neckline curve along the center front crease. Staystitch ½ inch from the cut edges to prevent stretching.

Step 9. Turn under and press 1¼ inches at the lower edge of the jacket. Turn under and press ¼ inch at the raw edge—or serge-finish the raw edge. Topstitch the hem in place close to the inner turned or serged edge.

Step 10. For the button tabs, cut three 3 x 5-inch rectangles from the dress fabric leftovers and from the fusible interfacing. Apply the interfacing to the wrong side of each 3 x 5-inch tab rectangle following manufacturer's directions. With right sides together, fold each piece in half, forming a 2½ x 3-inch rectangle. Stitch ½ inch from the both short edges. Trim the seams to ¼ inch, clip the corners and turn right side out. Press.

Step 11. With right sides together, pin the first tab to the right front jacket edge with the upper edge of the tab 1 inch below the neckline edge and the tab raw edges extending ¼ inch beyond the front edge. Place the upper edge of the next tab 3½ inches below the lower edge of the first one. Repeat this spacing for the remaining tab placement. Machine baste the tabs in place ⅛ inch from the jacket edge.

Step 12. Unfold and pin wide bias tape to the right side of the jacket at each center-front edge, allowing an extra ½ inch to extend at the bottom on each front edge. Stitch in place along the fold line of the bias tape. Trim the tab edges even with the jacket edge. Press the bias tape toward the seam allowance and understitch. Turn under the excess bias at the lower front edges and then turn the bias tape to the inside of the jacket. Pin in place and then topstitch close to the inner folded edge.

Step 13. Finish the jacket neckline with the narrower bias tape as directed in Step 12, allowing an extra ½ inch of tape to extend at each front edge as you did at the bottom edges.

Step 14. Make the jacket pockets as directed in Steps 11-14 for the dress. Position the pockets on the jacket front with the lower edge 3 inches from the lower edge of the jacket and 3 inches from the finished front edge. Topstitch in place.

Step 15. Make a buttonhole in the center of each tab and sew the large buttons in place under the tabs on the left jacket front.

Step 16. For cuffs, turn the lower edge of each sleeve up twice, adjusting the sleeves to the desired finished length.

INSTRUCTIONS
Shoulder Bag
Step 1. From the dress and the dress lining fabric, cut one 14 x 30-inch rectangle. For the inside pocket, cut one 10 x 11-inch rectangle from lining fabric. For the flap and tab, follow the cutting directions in Step 10 of the dress directions.

Step 2. Center the fusible interfacing on the wrong side of the lining rectangle and fuse in place following the manufacturer's directions.

Step 3. With the lining right side up, turn up 12 inches at the short bottom edge and crease the fold. Turn top edge down 5½ inches and crease the fold.

Step 4. Machine baste ½ inch from all edges of the inner pocket piece. Turn under the side and bottom edges along the basting and press; remove the basting. Turn under the upper edge and press, then turn the raw edge in to the fold and press. Stitch close to the inner folded edge. Unfold the lining and center the pocket on the lining with the lower edge along the crease as shown in Fig. 8. Edgestitch to the lining along the side and lower edges. Make bar tacks at the upper corners for reinforcement.

Step 5. With right sides together, pin the lining to the purse rectangle. Stitch ½ inch from the raw edges, leaving an opening in the lower edge for turning. Trim the seams to ¼ inch, clip the corners and turn right side out. Press. Slipstitch the opening closed.

Step 6. With the bag fabric on the inside, fold the bag along the creases in the lining. Pin the edges of the bag together and edgestitch the layers together, leaving a 1-inch-long opening at each lower corner. You will complete the seams after attaching the cording handle. Turn the bag right side out.

Step 7. Make an overhand knot about ½ inch from one end of the cord for the strap and tuck the raw end of the cord into the opening at one lower corner of the bag. Hand tack in place. Complete the seam on the inside, catching the cord end in the seam. You may need to use a zipper foot in order to stitch close enough to the edge.

Step 8. On the outside of bag, hand-sew the cord along the bag edge and, when you reach the upper edge, make a knot in the

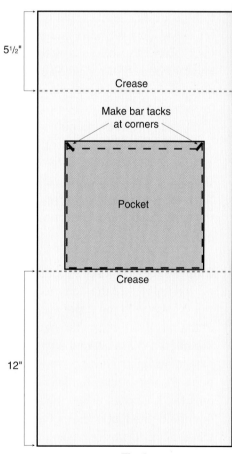

Fig. 8
Edgestitch pocket to lining right side.

cord and adjust it so that is at the flap fold line. Make another knot approximately 36 inches from the previous knot and position it at the flap fold on the opposite side of the bag. Hand-sew the remainder of the cord to the opposite edge of the bag. When you are close to the remaining bottom corner, make an overhand knot and adjust the position as needed. Tuck the raw end into the bag. Complete the seam at the corner as for the first one. Apply liquid seam sealant to the cord ends inside the bag.

Step 9. Prepare the tabbed flap following Steps 12-14 of the directions for the dress. Center the flap on the purse 1 inch above the finished edge and edgestitch in place. Attach a hook-and-loop dot closure to the underside of the flap and the bag. ■

Checkerboard Wrap Skirt

Stitch two simple seams, add a tie belt and you're ready to wrap this soft skirt over your favorite T-shirt, tank or swimsuit—easy dressing at its most comfortable.

DESIGN BY CAROL ZENTGRAF

PROJECT SPECIFICATIONS

Skill Level: Intermediate

Skirt Size: Any size

MATERIALS

Note: *Materials listed are for a Misses Medium with a finished length of 32 inches. Adjust yardage as needed for your size after determining the cutting dimensions as directed in Steps 1–3.*

- 2 yards 44/45-inch-wide, light- to medium-weight fabric such as rayon challis
- 3/8 yard lightweight fusible interfacing
- Water- or air-soluble marking pen
- All-purpose thread to match fabric
- Skirt/trouser hook and eye
- Cutting mat with 1-inch grid
- Tissue paper and pencil
- Basic sewing supplies and tools

INSTRUCTIONS

Project Note: *Use ¼-inch-wide seam allowances.*

Step 1. To determine your skirt size, use the following measurements (given in inches) as a guide:

	Small	Med.	Large	X-Large
Waist	25–27	28–30	31–35	36–39
Hips	34–36	37–40	41–44	45–48

Step 2. Fold the fabric in half lengthwise with right sides together and selvages aligned. Slip the cutting mat underneath to use as a guide. Referring to Fig. 1 and using the water- or air-soluble marking pen, draw the skirt back outline for your size on the fabric. Draw 5¼-inch-long dart lines as indicated for your size. Pin the

fabric layers together and cut out the skirt back.

Note: *The pattern diagrams include ¼-inch-wide seam allowances. For fabrics that ravel, add an extra ¼ inch to the waistline and front edges of the skirt pieces when cutting out and use ½-inch-wide seams.*

Step 3. Referring to Fig. 2, mark, pin, and cut the skirt fronts as you did for the skirt back.

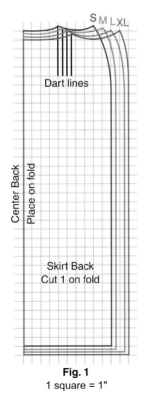

Fig. 1
1 square = 1"

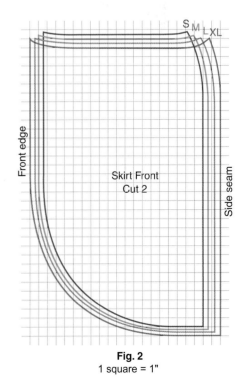

Fig. 2
1 square = 1"

Step 4. For the ties, cut four strips each 2¼ x 18 inches from the fabric and two strips of the same size from the fusible interfacing. Apply the interfacing to the wrong side of two of the fabric strips. With right sides together and using ¼-inch-wide seams, sew each interfaced strip to one of the remaining strips along one short edge and both long edges. Clip the corners and turn the strips right side out. Press. Edgestitch if desired.

Step 5. To make the darts, fold along the dart line and press. Beginning at the waistline edge and ⅞ inch from the dart fold, stitch a dart, gradually narrowing to a point at the end of the dart line. Press toward the center back.

Step 6. Pin the upper edge of the darted skirt back to a piece of tissue paper and trace the upper shaped edge and 3 inches on each side seam. Remove the skirt back and draw a cutting line to make the back facing pattern as shown in Fig. 3. Cut one back facing from the remaining skirt fabric and one from the fusible interfacing. Apply interfacing to the facing wrong side following manufacturer's directions.

Step 7. Make a facing pattern for the skirt front in the same manner. Cut two facings from the fabric and apply fusible interfacing. With right sides together, sew the front facings to the back facing at the side seams. Press the seams open. Finish the facing lower edge with serging or turn under and stitch ¼ inch to clean-finish.

Step 8. With raw edges even and right sides together, position a tie ½ inch below the upper cut edge of each skirt front as shown in Fig. 4. Baste in place.

Step 9. With right sides together, serge the skirt back to the fronts at the side seams and press the seam toward the skirt back. If you don't have a serger, stitch the seams and then zigzag the seam allowances together. Press.

Step 10. Serge-finish around the outer raw edges of the skirt from waistline edge to waistline edge. If you don't have a serger, zigzag-finish instead.

Step 11. With right sides together and keeping the ends of the ties out of the way of the stitching, sew the facing to the skirt upper and front edges as shown in Fig. 5. Clip the corners. Understitch along the upper edges, stitching as far into the front corners as possible so the facing will turn easily and smoothly to the inside. Turn and press, and then topstitch ¼ inch from the upper edge.

Step 12. Turn under and press ¼ inch around the outer edge of the skirt. Topstitch in place.

Step 13. Sew the eye of a skirt/trouser hook to the side seam allowance. Try the skirt on and tie in place. Mark the positioning for the hook on the skirt overlap and sew in place. ■

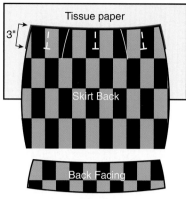

Fig. 3
Trace upper and side edges.

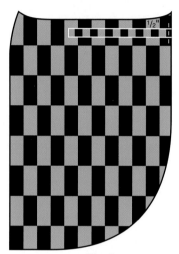

Fig. 4
Baste tie to skirt front edge.

Fig. 5
Stitch facing to waistline and front edges.

Beaded Chenille Poncho

Use unique beads to express your personal style when embellishing this softly structured poncho.

DESIGN BY LORI BLANKENSHIP

PROJECT SPECIFICATIONS
Skill Level: Beginner
Poncho Size: One size fits most

MATERIALS
- 2 yards 44-inch-wide woven chenille
- 1 skein coordinating yarn
- All-purpose thread to match fabric
- Glass beads
- Beading needle
- Large-eyed hand-sewing needle
- Rotary cutter, mat and ruler
- Glass-head pins
- Marking chalk
- 2 x 5-inch cardboard rectangle
- Basic sewing supplies and tools

INSTRUCTIONS
Step 1. From the chenille, cut a 34⅝ x 68-inch rectangle. Serge- or zigzag-finish all cut edges.

Step 2. With right sides together, fold the panel in half to measure 34 x 34⅝ inches. Beginning at the fold and using a ⅝-inch-wide seam, stitch from the fold to the raw edges on one side only. Turn right side out.

Step 3. Arrange the panel on a flat work surface and mark both raw edges at each corner for the wrist openings as shown in Fig. 1. *Note: The wrist openings will measure 30 inches between each set of marks.*

Step 4. Fold the poncho square in half lengthwise and chalk-mark the neckline opening as shown in Fig. 2. Cut on the line through all layers. Unfold the poncho. Serge- or zigzag-finish the neckline cut edge.

Step 5. To make tassels, wrap yarn around the 2-inch width of the cardboard rectangle five times. With the large-eyed hand-sewing needle, slip a 5-inch length of yarn through the top loops and tie a knot. Cut the bottom loops of the yarn along the edge of the

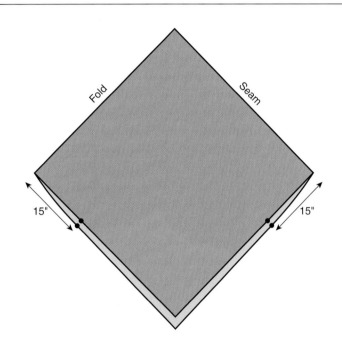

Fig. 1
Mark wrist openings.

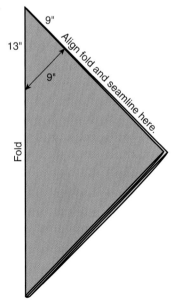

Fig. 2
Mark neck opening.

cardboard. Fold the yarn ends from the knot down and blend into the tassel. Wrap a second 5-inch length of yarn around the tassel 3/8 inch from tassel top and tie a knot as shown in Fig. 3. You will need approximately 62 tassels. Make more as needed.

Step 6. Turn under and press ¼ inch around the poncho neckline and outer edges. With a large-eyed hand-sewing needle and coordinating yarn, blanket-stitch over the turned edges, making alternating long and short stitches.

Step 7. To finish, hand-sew a yarn tassel to every other stitch along the poncho outer edges, as shown in Fig. 4. Note that there are no tassels around the wrist openings. Embellish the end of each stitch around the neckline with a glass bead as shown. Use a beading needle and strong thread. ■

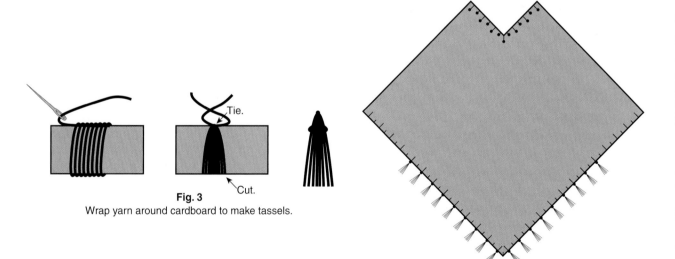

Fig. 3
Wrap yarn around cardboard to make tassels.

Fig. 4
Sew tassels to outer edges
and add beads around neckline.

Fleecy Fringed Poncho

This colorful poncho is easy to sew and fun to wear. Change the size of the square to create a poncho perfect for any size!

DESIGN BY NANCY FIEDLER

PROJECT SPECIFICATIONS
Skill Level: Beginner
Poncho Size: Yardage given is for a child's medium

MATERIALS
- 1 yard 60-inch-wide fleece
- ⅛ yard ribbing
- 4 yards ball fringe
- 4 yards flat trim (such as daisy chain, ribbon or jumbo rickrack)
- All-purpose thread to match fabric
- Air- or water-soluble marking pen
- 6-inch paper circle
- Basic sewing supplies and tools

INSTRUCTIONS
Project Note: Use ¼-inch-wide seam allowances.

Step 1. Cut a 33-inch square from the fleece.

Step 2. For the neck opening, find and mark the center of the fleece square. Center the circle template over the mark and draw around the template. Cut on the line.

Step 3. From the ribbing, cut a 6 x 12½-inch strip. With right sides facing, sew the ribbing short ends together. Turn right side out.

Step 4. Fold the ribbing in half lengthwise with wrong sides together and raw edges even. Divide and mark the ribbing in quarters.

Step 5. Fold the fleece square in half and then in half again to divide the neckline in fourths. Mark the folds. Unfold. With raw edges even, pin the ribbing to the neckline right side at the quarter-marks. The neckline will be larger than the ribbing as shown in Fig 1. Stitch the ribbing to the neckline, stretching it to fit the

poncho neckline opening as needed.

Step 6. Pin the flat trim in place 2 inches from the outer edge of the poncho. Stitch in place. Stitch the ball fringe to the outer edge of the poncho. ∎

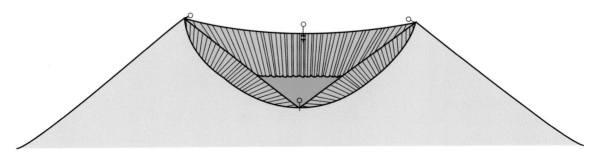

Fig. 1
Pin ribbing to poncho neckline, matching marks.

Snuggle Sack

Stay warm this winter in a cozy fleece snuggle sack. Cut from basic rectangles, this cuddly "sack" has cuffed openings for your feet that keep out the cold. If you'd rather have a warm robe, don't add the cuffs and hem the bottom edge instead.

DESIGN BY CAROL ZENTGRAF

PROJECT SPECIFICATIONS
Skill Level: Intermediate
Snuggle Sack Size: Small, medium, large and extra-large
Traditional Robe Size: Small, medium, large and extra-large

MATERIALS
Project Note: To determine the amount of ribbing required, add your wrist and ankle circumference and double the measurement for the required length. For the robe variation, double your wrist circumference.

- 2⅜ yards 60-inch-wide fleece for size small; 2⅞ yards for size medium; 3⅛ yards for size large or extra-large
- 2½–3-inch-wide coordinating folded ribbing in yardage determined above
- 4 Size 4 decorative snaps for robe
- 22-inch non-separating sports zipper
- All-purpose thread to match fabrics
- Water-soluble fabric marker
- Water-soluble, double-sided basting tape
- Basic sewing supplies and tools

INSTRUCTIONS
Snuggle Sack
Project Note: The cutting measurements are suggestions for average sizes based on half of the full-hip measurement plus 8–10 inches for seams and wearing ease. Adjust the width as needed to fit your figure. Use ¼-inch seam allowances throughout.

Fleece requires little if any pressing. If you must press, use a low temperature to avoid melting the fabric and press from the wrong side. Seam finishing is not necessary as the fabric does not ravel.

Step 1. For the sack front and back, cut two rectangles for your size: 17 x 55 inches for small ;

28 x 56 inches for medium; 30 x 57 inches for large; 32 x 57 inches for extra-large.

Step 2. For all sizes, cut one 6½ x 20½-inch strip for the collar and four 6 x 7-inch rectangles for the pockets. From the ribbing, cut two strips equal to your wrist measurement and two strips equal to your ankle measurement.

Step 3. With the fabric folded, use the marking pen to draw the cutting lines for the sleeves. Refer to Fig. 1 for the correct dimensions for your size. For each size increase, add ½ inch to all sleeve measurements for the size small as shown in Fig. 1.

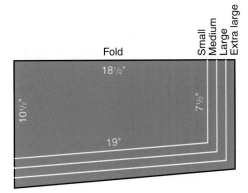

Fig. 1
For each size increase add ½" to all measurements as shown.

Step 4. For the front leg openings, draw arcs as shown in Fig. 2. Cut along the drawn lines. Repeat for the back leg openings.

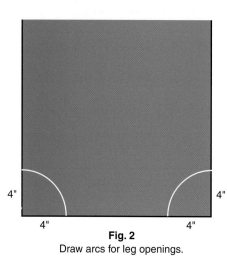

Fig. 2
Draw arcs for leg openings.

Step 5. Fold the front and back rectangles in half lengthwise and mark the neckline cutting lines as shown in Fig. 3. Cut along the lines. Mark the center of each neckline before unfolding.

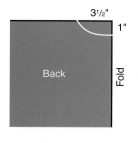

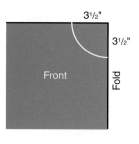

Fig. 3
Draw curves for back and front necklines.

Step 6. On the right front, draw a 22-inch-long line for the zipper opening at center front. Cut along the line. Make two angled ¼-inch-long clips at the base of the slit as shown in Fig. 4.

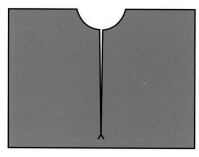

Fig. 4
Cut center front opening for zipper.

Step 7. Adhere basting tape along both edges on the right side of the zipper tape. With the zipper pull facing you, remove the backing from the right-hand zipper tape and place it face down on the left side of the zipper opening with the zipper tape edge even with the fabric edge. The zipper pull should be ¾ inch below the neckline edge and the zipper bottom stop should be at the bottom of the opening. Beginning at the lower end of the zipper, stitch ¼ inch from the zipper-tape edge as shown in Fig. 5. Sew the remaining half of the zipper to the remaining raw edge.

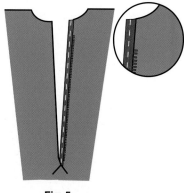

Fig. 5
Sew zipper to left front ¼" from edge.

Step 8. At the bottom end of the finished zipper, tuck the little triangle of fabric inside and hand sew to the zipper tape.

Step 9. Fold the collar in half lengthwise with right sides together and stitch the short ends together. Turn right side out and machine-baste the long edges together. Mark the center of the basted edge.

Step 10. With right sides together, sew the front and back together at the shoulder seams. Turn right side out. Unzip the zipper. With centers and raw edges matching and the front edges even, pin the collar to the neckline. Stitch.

Step 11. Mark the center of each sleeve upper edge. With right sides together and the sleeve center at the shoulder seam, pin and stitch the sleeves to the sack.

Step 12. Pin the pockets to the garment with right sides together and the upper pocket edge 9½ inches below the sleeve underarm edge. Stitch. Turn each pocket out over the seam allowance. Refer to Fig. 6 on page 123.

Step 13. With right sides together and raw edges even, pin the front and back together along the side and underarm seams as shown in Fig. 6. Stitch.

Step 14. Stitch the bottom edges together from leg hole to leg hole.

Step 15. To make each cuff, open the folded ribbing and fold in half with short ends even. Stitch. Refold with the seam inside and the raw edges even.

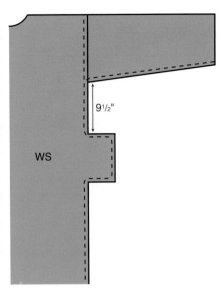

Fig. 6
Stitch underarm, side seams & pockets.

Step 16. With right sides together and raw edges even, pin and stitch each cuff to the appropriate opening edge, stretching the ribbing if necessary to fit the opening as you stitch.

Step 17. Following the manufacturer's directions, apply a decorative snap to each corner of the collar and the corresponding point on the snuggle sack. Apply a snap to the center of each pocket.

Traditional Robe

Project Note: *Measure from the top of your shoulder down to the desired robe length and add 1 inch for the hem allowance. Use this measurement to adjust the rectangle length for your size. Cut ribbing for wrist cuffs only. Use ¼-inch-wide seam allowances.*

Step 1. Follow instructions for making the Snuggle Sack, omitting Steps 4 and 14.

Step 2. To finish the robe, turn under a 1-inch-wide hem at the lower edges and topstitch in place ¼ inch from the cut edge. ∎

Suede-Trimmed Wool Jacket

This casual, loose-fitting jacket features a suede collar and front band for a touch of elegance. Use the "real thing" or substitute nonwoven synthetic suede for the collar.

DESIGN BY CAROL ZENTGRAF

PROJECT SPECIFICATIONS

Skill Level: Confident beginner

Finished Size: Your size based on your measurements

MATERIALS

- 2¼ yards 54-inch-wide wool
- 2 (8 x 36-inch) strips of real suede or ½ yard synthetic suede
- Dressmaker's chalk or marking pencil
- Leather sewing machine needle if using real suede; universal sewing machine needle for synthetic suede
- Rotary cutter, mat and ruler
- All-purpose thread to match fabric
- Teflon or walking foot for the sewing machine
- For synthetic suede: ¼-inch-wide and ½-inch-wide strips of paper-backed fusible web and a press cloth
- Permanent fabric adhesive
- Basic sewing supplies

INSTRUCTIONS

Project Note: *Using ½-inch-wide seam allowances, sew all seams with right sides together.*

Step 1. To determine your size for cutting purposes, use the following full-hip measurements as a guide: small, 34 to 36 inches; medium: 37 to 40 inches and large, 41 to 44 inches.

Step 2. Fold the jacket fabric in half with right sides together and selvages matching. Referring to Fig. 1, use dressmaker's chalk and a ruler to measure and mark the cutting lines for your size on the fabric. Cut out the jacket body and make a ¹/₈-inch-long snip at the center-back fold. Snip-mark the center of the raw edge of the armhole in the same manner.

Step 3. Referring to Fig. 2 on page 127, cut two sleeves. Fold the sleeve in half lengthwise and snip ¹/₈ inch at the fold along the upper edge to mark the shoulder placement.

Step 4. From the suede or synthetic suede, cut two strips each 8 x 36 inches. **Note:** *You will cut them to the appropriate length for your size later.*

Step 5. Arrange the suede strips side by side

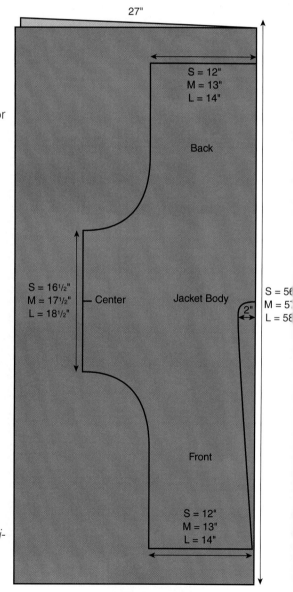

Fig. 1
Mark and cut jacket
from the wool.

and run your hand in one direction. If both strips do not both feel smooth in that direction, reverse the position of one strip so they do.

Step 6. Attach the Teflon or walking foot to the sewing machine. For real suede only, change to a leather sewing machine needle. Sew the upper short ends of the strips together to make one long collar/front band. Finger-press the seam open and trim to ¼ inch. Use permanent fabric adhesive between the seam allowance and the collar band to hold the leather seam open, or tuck a narrow strip of fusible web between the collar and the seam allowances of a synthetic suede collar and fuse the seam allowance in place. Use a press cloth to protect the fabric.

Step 7. On a real suede collar, apply the adhesive to the wrong side along one long edge. Turn under ½ inch and use your fingers to "press" it in place. For synthetic suede, apply a ½-inch strip of fusible web to the wrong side of one long edge following the manufacturer's directions. Remove the backing paper and turn under ½ inch. Fuse, using a press cloth to protect the fabric. Topstitch ¼ inch from the turned edge.

Step 8. With right sides together and the center back seam at the clip mark for the center back, pin the collar to the jacket back and front neckline edges. Stitch from the center back to the lower edge to attach each half of the collar to the jacket. Trim the excess suede even with the lower front edges of the jacket. Finger-press the seam allowance toward the jacket and topstitch through all layers ¼ inch from the seam line. On the inside, use fabric adhesive to glue the turned and topstitched edge of the suede to the seam allowance.

Step 9. With right sides together and the center snips matching, sew or serge a sleeve to each armhole edge. If you sew the seam, finish the seam allowances together with a narrow zigzag stitch. Press the seam toward the jacket.

Step 10. With right sides together and the armhole seams matching, pin and serge or stitch the jacket underarm and side seam in one long seam as shown in Fig. 3. Finish the seam edges with zig-zagging if you stitched rather than serged the seams. Press serged seams toward the jacket and sleeve back. Press stitched seams open.

Step 11. Finish the jacket and sleeve raw edges with serging or zigzagging. Turn under and press a 1-inch-wide hem at the lower edge of the jacket. Topstitch ¾ inch from the lower pressed edge. Try on the jacket and roll the sleeves to create a deep double cuff, adjusting the length as needed. There is no need to hem the lower edge of the sleeve. ■

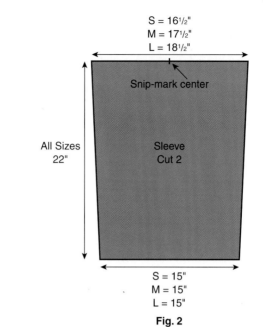

S = 16½"
M = 17½"
L = 18½"

Snip-mark center

All Sizes
22"

Sleeve
Cut 2

S = 15"
M = 15"
L = 15"

Fig. 2
Mark and cut 2 sleeves from the wool.

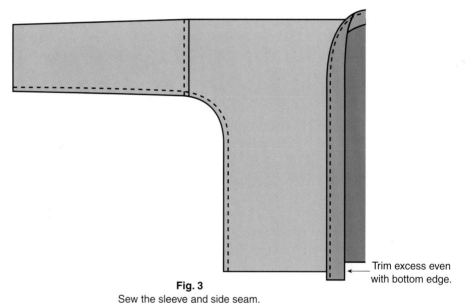

Trim excess even with bottom edge.

Fig. 3
Sew the sleeve and side seam.

All-Occasion Sweatshirt Jacket

Turn a sweatshirt into a head-turning jacket with a few simple snips and colorful fabric accents.

DESIGN BY MARIAN SHENK

PROJECT SPECIFICATIONS

Skill Level: Intermediate
Sweatshirt Size: Desired size; jacket should be loose fitting.

MATERIALS

Yardage given is for 44/45-inch-wide cotton fabrics for a large-size sweatshirt. You may need less fabric for smaller sizes. Preshrink the sweatshirt and the fabrics before you begin sewing to ensure washability later.
For reference only, the colors used in the sample are given in parentheses in the list.

- Sweatshirt in a color and size of your choice (navy)
- 1 yard border-striped fabric in coordinating colors (blue and red)
- ¾ yard coordinating tone-on-tone print #1 (blue)
- ⅞ yard coordinating tone-on-tone print #2 (red)
- ⅛ yard coordinating floral print (blue and red) for the pocket and back medallion patchwork
- ½ yard muslin for the pocket and back medallion foundation
- 1 yard thin cotton batting
- All-purpose thread to match fabric
- Optional: Walking foot or built-in even-feed feature on your machine
- Rotary cutter, mat and ruler
- Basic sewing supplies and tools

INSTRUCTIONS

Project Note: *Use ½-inch-wide seam allowances.*

Step 1. Trim away the cuff, neckband and bottom band of the sweatshirt. Align the side seams to locate the center front and press. Cut on the crease. Referring to Fig. 1, cut off the upper corner on each front to shape the neckline.

Fig. 1
Cut sweatshirt open at center front and reshape neckline.

Step 2. From the border stripe, cut strips 5 inches wide. Sew the strips together, end to end, to make one long piece. Take care to match the motifs. Press the seams open.

Note: *You may need to vary the strip width to accommodate the width of the border stripe in your fabric. Allow for ½-inch-wide seams. The finished bottom and neckline bands should measure approximately 4 inches wide but may be wider or narrower depending on how you cut the border-stripe strips.*

Step 3. Taking care not to stretch the fabric, measure the lower edge of the sweatshirt and cut a strip from the border stripe this length. Cut a 5-inch-wide strip of batting and of coordinating tone-on-tone print #1 (blue) for the band facing to match this length.

Step 4. Baste the batting strip to the wrong side of the border strip. With right sides facing, pin the border stripe strip to the sweatshirt lower edge. Pin the right side of the band facing of print #1 to the wrong side of the sweatshirt, sandwiching the shirt between the two bands.

Step 5. If available, attach a walking foot or engage the even-feed feature on your machine. Using a ½-inch-wide seam allowance, stitch the bottom bands and batting to the sweatshirt. Trim the

seam allowance to ¼ inch and press the bands toward the seam allowance as shown in Fig. 2.

Step 6. Measure the length of the back neckline and center-front edges of the sweatshirt, including the bottom band. Cut a strip this length from the border stripe, batting and print #1 (blue). Baste the batting to the wrong side of the border stripe.

Step 7. With right sides together, pin the strip of print #1 (blue) to the neckline and front edges. Pin the batting-backed border stripe to the sweatshirt with the right side of the print against the wrong side of the sweatshirt. *Note: This is the reverse of how bands were sewn to the bottom edge.* Stitch ½ inch from the raw edges. Trim and press as directed for the bottom band.

Step 8. Sew all layers together around the outer edges of the sweatshirt. Use a basting-length stitch and sew ³/₈ inch from the raw edges as shown in Fig. 3.

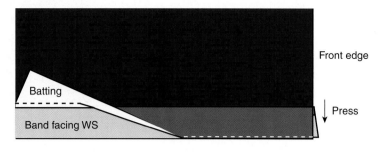

Fig. 2
Stitch bottom band and batting to sweatshirt.

3 inches wide. Cut strips across the fabric grain. Using bias seams as shown in Fig. 4, sew the strips together to make one long piece of binding. Press the seams open. Fold the strip in half lengthwise with wrong sides together and press.

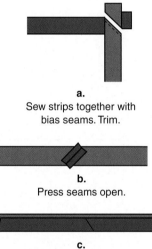

a.
Sew strips together with bias seams. Trim.

b.
Press seams open.

c.
Fold strips in half; press.
Fig. 4
Prepare binding.

Step 10. Pin binding to the bottom edge of the jacket and stitch ½ inch from the raw edges. Press the binding toward the seam allowance and wrap to the inside. Slipstitch in place along the seam line.

Step 11. Repeat Step 9 to bind the raw edges of the neckline band. Sew the binding to the striped side and slipstitch in place on the band facing.

Step 12. Turn the neckline band back onto the jacket along the seam line and pin in place for 20 inches from the lower edge on each front. Stitch in the ditch of the binding seam in the pinned area to anchor the band to the jacket as shown in Fig. 5.

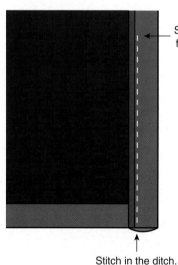

Stop stitching from lower ed

Stitch in the ditch.

Fig. 5
Stitch in the ditch to attach the band to the jacket.

Step 13. Measure the lower edge of the sleeve and add 1 inch for seams. Cut two 4½-inch-wide strips of the border stripe, batting and print #1 (blue) for the cuffs and cuff facings. Baste the batting to the wrong side of the border-stripe bands. With right sides facing and raw edges aligned, stitch the short ends of each band together. Repeat with the band

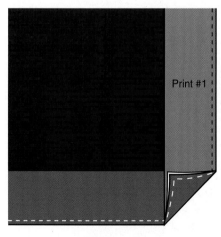

Print #1

Fig. 3
Baste all raw edges together.

Step 9. From tone-on-tone print #2 (red), cut five strips, each facing. Trim the seam in the facings to ¼ inch and press open. Trim the batting close to the stitching in the border-stripe cuffs. Press the seam open.

Step 14. With right sides together and seam lines matching, pin a print #1 (blue) facing to the lower edge of each sleeve. Pin a striped cuff to the sleeve edge with the right side of the stripe against the wrong side of the cuff as for the front band. Stitch ½ inch from the raw edges and trim the seam to ¼ inch. Press the bands and facings toward the seam allowance as shown in Fig. 6.

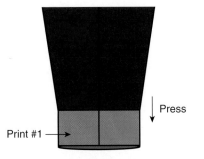

Fig. 6
Press the sleeve band toward the seam allowance.

Step 15. Bind the cuff lower edge, stitching the binding to the border stripe side of the cuff and slipstitching it to the facing side. Turn the cuff to the outside of the sleeve and adjust as desired.

Step 16. For the pockets and the back medallion, cut six 8-inch squares from the batting and muslin. From print #1, cut three 8-inch squares. Crosscut diagonally from corner to corner to make six triangles.

Step 17. Cut one 2¼-inch-wide strip from each of prints #2 and #3 and from the border stripe. Cut the strips across the fabric width.

Step 18. Position each batting square on top of a muslin square. Place a print #1 triangle at one corner of each square on top of the batting. Pin in place. With right

sides together, stitch the border stripe strip to the long raw edge of the triangle on each square. Press the strip away from the triangle. Add a strip of the floral print next, followed by a strip of print #2. Press the completed squares. Trim each piece of patchwork to 7½ inches square as shown in Fig. 7.

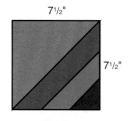

7½"

7½"

Fig. 7
Make four pieced squares.

Step 19. To make the back medallion, arrange four squares in two rows with the red corners meeting in the center. Stitch the squares together in rows and trim the seams to ¼ inch. Press the seams open. Sew the two rows together as shown in Fig. 8.

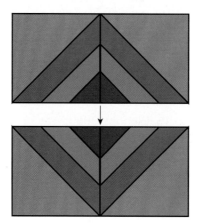

Fig. 8
Sew squares together for back medallion.

Step 20. Bind the outer edge of the completed square with print #2. Bind the outer edges of the remaining squares for the pockets.

Step 21. Center the medallion on the jacket back, placing it on point. Pin in place. Stitch in the ditch of the binding seam all around the medallion.

Step 22. Pin the pockets in place on the jacket fronts, just inside the front and bottom bands with the red corners at the bottom toward the center front. Stitch in the ditch along the side and bottom edges of each pocket. Backstitch at the pocket upper edges for added security. Press. ■

Lined Denim Tote

Here's a great way to use up denim scraps and turn them into an interesting and durable shoulder tote.

DESIGN BY JUNE FIECHTER

PROJECT SPECIFICATIONS

Skill Level: Confident beginner
Tote Size: Approximately 3 x 13¼ x 13¼ inches, excluding handle

MATERIALS

- Denim scraps (at least 8 inches square) or ½ yard 44/45-inch-wide denim
- ½ yard 44/45-inch-wide coordinating fabric for lining
- 1 yard heavyweight fusible interfacing
- 2 (1-inch) squares hook-and-loop tape
- Liquid seam sealant
- Embellishing glue
- 2⅔ yards #8 Kreinik polyester metallic fine braid (Gun Metal #011HL)
- 1 (¾-inch) blue button
- All-purpose thread to match fabrics
- Pinking shears and dressmaker's shears
- Pencil and paper
- Hand-sewing needle
- Basic sewing supplies and tools

INSTRUCTIONS

Step 1. To make the petal template, refer to Fig. 1. Draw and cut out a 3 x 5½-inch paper rectangle. Fold in half lengthwise. With the fold to the left, draw a half-teardrop shape with the point beginning at bottom left-hand corner. Draw another line inside the first one and ⅝ inch from it. Cut out the teardrop on both lines to create a hollow teardrop template.

Step 2. Using pinking shears, cut eight 6¾-inch squares for the tote bag front and back, two strips each 3 x 20 inches for the tote side/bottom panel and one 3 x 30-inch strip for the strap.

Step 3. Using the paper template from Step 1, trace four petals on the wrong side of a piece of denim. Cut out the petals using the dressmaker's shears. Apply liquid seam sealant to all raw edges and set petals aside to dry.

Step 4. From coordinating fabric for the lining, cut two 13½-inch squares for the tote front and back, two 3 x 20-inch strips for

the side/bottom panel, and one 2½ x 30-inch strip for the strap. Cut matching pieces from the fusible interfacing. Apply the interfacing to the lining wrong side following the manufacturer's directions.

Step 5. Arrange 4 denim squares for the front, overlapping them ⅜ inch at the center edges to create a large square. Topstitch together ¼ inch from the overlapping edges as shown in Fig. 2. Repeat for the tote back.

Step 6. Referring to the photo for placement, arrange the petals on the tote front with each point ⅜ inch from the center where the corners meet. Following the manufacturer's direction, attach the teardrops to the denim with embellishing glue. Set aside to dry

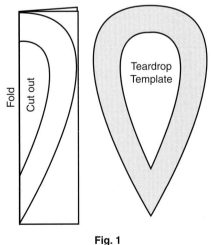

Fig. 1
Draw a line ⅝" inside the outer curved line.

Fig. 2
Topstitch together ¼" from overlapped edges.

Step 7. Using a ³⁄₈-inch-wide seam, sew the side/bottom lining strips together at one set of short ends. Press the seam open. Serge-finish the long edges with a medium-width, medium length 3- or 4-thread stitch. If you do not have a serger, zigzag-finish the edges or apply a thin line of seam sealant to the long raw edges and allow to dry thoroughly.

Step 8. With right sides together and raw edges even, pin the lining side/bottom panel to the side and bottom edges of one 13½-inch lining square. Clip the tote as needed to turn the corners, making the clips a scant ³⁄₈ inch long. Stitch together, using a ³⁄₈-inch-wide seam allowance. Repeat with the remaining lining square. At the upper edge of the lining, turn under and press ¼ inch.

Step 9. Lap the short end of one denim side/bottom panel ³⁄₈ inch over the end of the other panel to make one long piece. Topstitch ¼ inch from the overlapped edge.

Step 10. Machine-baste ¼ inch from each long edge of the 3 x 20-inch denim strap. With the denim strap face down on the work surface, center the lining strap in place with right side up. Pin in place. Stitch ⅛ inch from the lining edges. Remove the basting.

Step 11. *Make sure the embellishing glue is dry before proceeding.* Using a hand-sewing needle

threaded with fine metallic braid, blanket-stitch around the inner and outer edges of each petal. Sew the button in place for the flower center.

Step 12. With wrong sides together pin the denim side/bottom panel to the bag front. Stitch ¼ inch from the raw edges. Repeat with the tote back.

Step 13. With wrong sides together, insert the lining in the tote. Pin in place with the turned edge of the lining slightly below the upper pinked edge of the tote. Stitch in place ⅛ inch from the lining edge.

Step 14. Position one short end of the strap on the side panel with the edge ¾ inch below the upper edge of the tote. Topstitch ¼ inch and again ½ from the strap edge. Repeat with the remaining end of the strap.

Step 15. Pin squares of hook-and-loop tape to the inside of the tote front, ½ inch below the upper edge and 4¾ inches in from the side seams. Topstitch in place close to the outer edges of each square. Repeat for the tote back. ∎

Tote Bag Trio

Travel in style with this trio of trendy tote bags. The roomy, zip-top duffle, handy tote and matching cosmetic bag are all easy to sew using reversible quilted fabrics with an unquilted border stripe or print coordinate for the trim.

DESIGN BY CAROL ZENTGRAF

PROJECT SPECIFICATIONS
Skill Level: Confident beginner
Duffle Bag Size: 11 x 11 x 22 inches
Tote Bag Size: 9 x 11 x 14 inches
Cosmetic Bag Size: 7 x 10 inches

MATERIALS

DUFFLE BAG
Note: All yardage is for 44/45-inch-wide fabric.

- 2 yards reversible quilted fabric
- ¾ yard coordinating unquilted fabric (Choose a border print, if available; otherwise an allover print will work.)
- 22-inch-long separating sport zipper with plastic teeth
- ¼-inch-wide fusible web
- All-purpose thread
- Rotary cutter, mat and ruler
- Basic sewing supplies

INSTRUCTIONS
Duffle Bag
Project Note: Use ½-inch-wide seam allowances throughout and sew all seams with right sides together. After sewing, trim all seams to ¼ inch and finish with narrow zigzagging or serging.

Step 1. From the quilted fabric, cut two 22 x 24-inch panels, two 12-inch squares, two 9 x 12-inch pocket pieces and two 3½ x 68-inch strips for the straps. Referring to Fig. 1, trim the 12-inch squares to make shaped end panels.

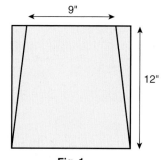

Fig. 1
Trim to reshape the tote end panels.

Step 2. From the unquilted coordinate, cut two strips each 4½ x 43 inches long. If using a border-print stripe, customize the width of the strip as desired, allowing for ½-inch-wide seam allowances beyond the desired "stripe."

Step 3. Finish one long edge of each 9 x 12-inch pocket piece with zigzagging or serging. Turn under and press a 1¼-inch-wide hem. Topstitch ¼, ½ and ¾ inches from the folded edge.

Step 4. With the lower edges aligned, position a trimmed cut end panel on top of a hemmed pocket rectangle and trim the side edges to match as shown in Fig. 2. Fold each end panel in half lengthwise and snip mark the center at the top and bottom edges.

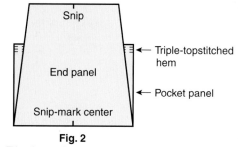

Fig. 2
Trim the pocket to match the end panel shape.

Step 5. With raw edges even, baste each pocket to an end panel along the side and bottom edges (Fig 3).

Fig. 3
Baste pocket to end panel along side and bottom edges.

Step 6. With right sides facing, sew the two large panels together along one 24-inch edge. Press the seam open. (You may serge the seam if you prefer and press it to one side.) Place the panel right side up on a large flat surface.

Step 7. Adhere a strip of fusible web along one long edge on the wrong side of each 43-inch-long strip. Remove the paper, turn under and press ½ inch, fusing it in place.

Step 8. Position a border strip face up on the right side of the tote panel with long raw edges even. Pin in place. Stitch the pressed edge of each strip in place as shown in Fig. 4.

Turn under ½"

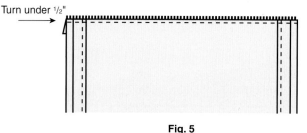

Fig. 5
Topstitch the tote to the zipper at both ends of the tote panel.

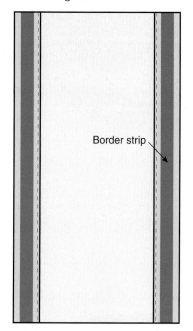

Fig. 4
Stitch the border strips in place.

Step 9. Turn under and press ½ inch at each short end of the tote panel. Unzip and separate the zipper. Position the pressed edges of the tote next to the zipper teeth and topstitch ¼ inch from the pressed edges as shown in Fig. 5.

Step 10. Sew the short ends of the 3½-inch-wide strips for the straps together using ¼-inch-wide seams to create a circle. Press the seams open. Turn under and press ½ inch on each long edge of the circular strip. Fold the strip in half with wrong sides together and turned edges even. Use fusible web to fuse the turned edges together. Stitch ⅛ inch from both long edges of each strap. Stitch ⅝ inch from one long edge through the center of each strap.

Step 11. With the strap seam lines matching the bottom seam and the outer edges ½ inch from the border edge, pin the straps in place. Stitching on top of all three rows of the previous stitching in the straps, sew the straps to the tote. End the stitching and back-stitching 6 inches from the zipper as shown in Figure 6.

Step 12. Zip the zipper and turn the tote panel wrong side out. With right sides together, pin an end panel to the tote end nearest the zipper slide, matching the snip marks to the bottom seam and the zipper center. Stitch. Serge or zigzag finish the seam edges as desired.

Step 13. Unzip the zipper, leaving the last several inches zipped. Pin and stitch the remaining end panel to the tote. Unzip the zipper and turn the tote right side out.

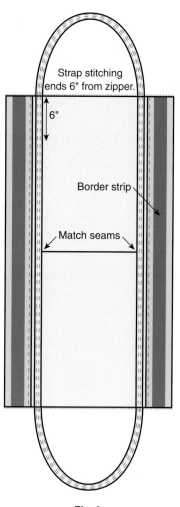

Strap stitching ends 6" from zipper.

6"

Border strip

Match seams

Fig. 6
Duffle Assembly

TOTE BAG

Note: *All yardage is for 44/45-inch-wide fabric.*

- ⅔ yard reversible quilted fabric
- 1⅛ yards coordinating unquilted fabric with vertical border stripe, or ⅛ yard of an allover print for the tote band trim
- ¼-inch-wide fusible web
- All-purpose thread to match fabrics
- Rotary cutter, mat and ruler
- Basic sewing supplies

INSTRUCTIONS
Tote Bag

Project Note: *Use ½-inch-wide seam allowances throughout and sew all seams with right sides together. After sewing, trim all seams to ¼ inch and finish with a narrow zigzag stitch or serging.*

Step 1. From the quilted fabric, cut two 15½ x 20-inch panels, two 5½ x 11-inch bottom rectangles, one 9 x 12-inch inside pocket rectangle and two 3½ x 24-inch strips for straps.

Step 2. From the border stripe or allover print for the upper band trim, cut one 4½ x 39-inch strip. If using a border print stripe, customize the width of the strip as desired, allowing for ½-inch-wide seam allowances beyond the desired "stripe."

Step 3. Serge-finish one 9-inch edge and both long edges of the pocket rectangle. Turn under and press 1 inch so the contrasting side of the fabric shows on the pocket right side as shown in Fig. 7. Topstitch in place.

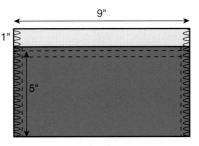

Fig. 7
Fold pocket as shown and stitch.

Step 4. Fold the pocket as shown in Fig. 7 and stitch ¼ inch from the serged edges. Turn right side out and press.

Step 5. Center the pocket at the upper short edge on the inside of one tote panel and use a strip of fusible web to "baste" it in place.

Step 6. Turn under and press ½ inch on each long edge of each 3½-inch strap. Fold each strap in half with wrong sides together and turned edges even. Use fusible web to fuse the turned edges together. Stitch ⅛ inch from both long edges of each strap. Stitch ⅝ inch from one long edge through the center of each strap.

Step 7. Position the raw ends of each strap on the inside of a tote panel as shown in Fig. 8 with the inner strap edges 6½ inches apart. Pin in place.

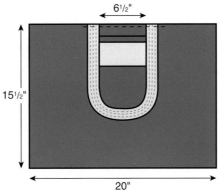

Fig. 8
Baste the straps to the upper edge on inside of each tote panel.

Step 8. Serge or sew one side seam of the tote. Press the seam open or to one side. Staystitch a scant ½ inch from the lower long raw edge of the panel. Place the tote wrong side up on a flat surface.

Step 9. Adhere a strip of fusible web along one long edge on the wrong side of the 4½-inch-wide upper-edge trim. Remove the paper and turn under and press ½ inch, fusing it in place.

Step 10. With the handles and pocket sandwiched between the trim and tote, position the right side of the strip face down on the inside of the tote panel. Align the raw edges and pin in place. Stitch ½ inch from the raw edges. Trim the seam to ¼ inch. Turn the trim to the right side of the tote panel and press as shown in Fig. 9. Topstitch ¼ inch from both edges of the trim.

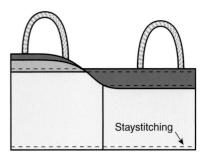

Staystitching

Fig. 9
Turn the trim to the outside and topstitch ¼" from both edges.

Step 11. With right sides together and side seams matching the bottom seam, pin the bottom to the tote. Clip the tote seam allowance as needed to round the corners as shown in Fig. 10 on page 140. Serge or sew. Trim the corners even with the tote raw edges.

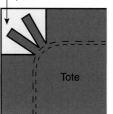

Fig. 10
Clip the tote to the staystitching to
turn the corners smoothly.

Step 12. To create a ridge around
the bottom for added stability, fold
the tote along the seam line and
topstitch ⅛ inch from the edge.

MATERIALS

COSMETIC BAG

Note: *All yardage is for 44/45-inch-
wide fabric.*

- ¼ yard reversible quilted fabric
- 3½ x 21-inch strip of coordinating
  unquilted fabric
- 9-inch piece of ¾-inch-wide
  hook-and-loop tape
- All-purpose thread to match fabrics
- Rotary cutter, mat and ruler
- Basic sewing supplies

INSTRUCTIONS
Cosmetic Bag

Project Note: *Use ½-inch-wide
seam allowances throughout
unless otherwise noted. Sew all
seams with right sides together.
After sewing, trim all seams to
¼ inch and finish with a narrow
zigzag stitch or serging.*

Step 1. From the quilted fabric,
cut two 8 x 11-inch rectangles.

Step 2. On the inside of each
quilted rectangle, center and stitch
a piece of the hook-and-loop tape
¾ inch from one long raw edge.

Step 3. With right sides facing,
serge or sew the two rectangles
together along the side and lower
edges. Do not turn right side out.

Step 4. Sew the short ends of the
3½-wide strips together and trim
seams to ¼ inch. Press open. Turn
under and press ½ inch at one
long edge of the piece. Turn the
raw edge into the fold and press.

Fig. 11
Edgestitch through all layers
at the upper edge of the cosmetic bag.

Stitch close to the inner folded
edge to make a narrow hem.

Step 5. Pin the trim band to the
upper raw edge of the bag with
the trim right side against the
wrong side of the cosmetic case
and raw edges even. Stitch. Trim
the seam to ¼ inch and press the
band toward the seam allowance.
Turn the band to the right side
of the bag and press. Topstitch
⅛ inch from the upper finished
edge as shown in Fig. 11. The trim
creates an upper cuff that is not
anchored at the lower raw edge. ∎

Casual Drawstring Shoulder Bag

Embroidered microfiber fabric is a unique choice for this soft, gathered shoulder bag. Choose a wonderful fabric and stitch one up in an afternoon.

DESIGN BY CARLA SCHWAB

PROJECT SPECIFICATIONS

Skill Level: Beginner
Shoulder Bag Size:
Approximately 7 x 14 x 7 inches

MATERIALS

- 1 yard decorative, light- to medium-weight fabric for bag
- 1 yard coordinating cotton print fabric for lining
- 3 yards cord for strap
- 2 (8-inch) squares heavy interfacing
- 3 yards $^3/_{16}$-inch-wide corded piping
- 2 ¼-inch-diameter buttons (optional)
- 28 ($^3/_8$-inch) metal grommets Grommet setting tool
- 2 (1-inch-diameter) buttons
- All-purpose thread to match fabrics
- 20-inch length of string
- Pencil
- 7¾-inch circle template
- 7-inch circle template
- Zipper foot
- Masking tape
- Basic sewing supplies and tools

INSTRUCTIONS

Step 1. Fold the lining in half crosswise with raw edges even, and then in half again crosswise so the resulting piece is approximately 18 x 22 inches. Place on a padded work surface. Tie one end of the string to a pencil. Measure 16¾ inches out from the pencil and tie a knot in the string at that point. Slip a large sewing pin through the knot and anchor it to the cutting surface at the folded corner of the folded fabric. Pull the string taut and draw the circle on the fabric. Cut out. Before unfolding the circle, mark the lining center. Cut four 6½ x 8-inch rectangles for the inside pockets.

Step 2. Use the lining circle as a pattern to cut a matching circle from the bag fabric. From the bag fabric, also cut one 7¾-inch-diameter circle for the bag inner bottom and mark the center.

Step 3. From the heavy interfacing, cut two 7-inch circles for the bag inner bottom. Baste the two interfacing circles together and mark the center. With centers matching, place the interfacing circles to the wrong side of the bag circle. Turn the raw edges over the interfacing and baste in place.

Step 4. With centers matching and the interfaced side of the circle against the right side of the large lining circle, stitch the circle in place close to the outer edge as shown in Fig. 1.

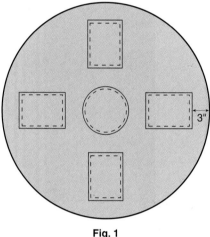

Fig. 1
Stitch circle and pockets to lining.

Step 5. Finish all four edges of each pocket by turning and pressing a double ¼-inch-wide hem. Stitch close to the inner edge on one short edge of each pocket.

Step 6. Position and pin the pockets in place on the lining as shown in Fig. 1. Place the open edge of each pocket 3 inches from and toward the outer edge of the lining circle. Stitch in place close to the side and bottom edges.

Step 7. Attach the zipper foot and machine-baste the corded piping in place along the outer edge of the bag circle, overlapping ends as shown in Fig. 2.

Step 8. With right sides together, stitch the bag to the lining, leaving a 4-inch opening for turning. Turn the bag right side out and press. Slipstitch the opening closed.

Step 9. Mark grommet spacing every 3½ inches around the outer edge of the bag about 1 inch from the finished edge (Fig. 3). Apply grommets to the outside of the bag following package directions. ***Note:*** *It's a good idea to test the* grommets on scraps of your fabric and lining. To ensure success on some fabrics, it may be necessary to make starter holes for the grommets using an awl or the sharp points of a small scissors.

Step 10. Cut the cord for the drawstring into two equal lengths. Wrap masking tape around the end of one length of cord to make it easier to thread through the grommets. Thread through the grommets, remove the tape and knot both ends, catch the cord ends between two buttons to prevent them from slipping through the grommets.

Step 11. Form a 1¾-inch-long loop at each end of the remaining piece of cord and hand sew in place. Loop the cord through the drawstring cord between two grommets as shown in Fig. 4.

Step 12. Sew buttons to the bag just above the stitching around the bottom circle, spacing them 3½ inches apart. Align them with the grommets directly above them through which the cord is looped. Position the loops around the buttons. ∎

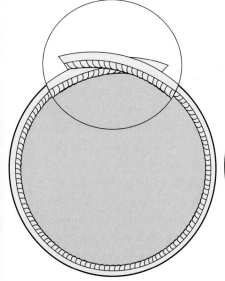

Fig. 2
Machine-baste corded piping to outer edge of bag, overlapping ends. Trim excess piping.

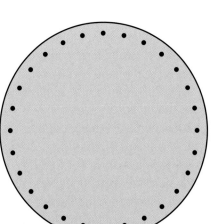

Fig. 3
Space grommets 3¹⁄₂" apart around outer edge.

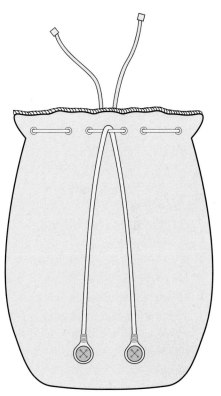

Fig. 4
Loop cord around drawstring between two grommets. Loop cord ends over buttons.

Spring Garden Tote Bag

For a touch of spring all year 'round, make this garden tote to carry your supplies and hand tools while you work in your flower garden. Or use it as a tote for shopping and errands.

DESIGN BY DEBRA QUARTERMAIN

PROJECT SPECIFICATIONS

Skill Level: Intermediate

Bag Size: Approximately 3 x 11½ x 17 inches, excluding handles

MATERIALS

- ¾ yard of 44/45-inch-wide large floral print for tote bag body
- ½ yard 44/45-inch-wide solid or print for lining
- 1 fat quarter multi-colored striped fabric for trim and straps
- 1 fat quarter small geometric print fabric for flowerpots, strap and pocket trim
- 5 x 12-inch floral fabric scrap for flowers
- 4 x 8-inch green print fabric scrap for leaves and stems
- ⅓ yard ¼-inch-wide satin ribbon
- Permanent fabric adhesive or narrow strips of fusible web
- 2 (⅞-inch) flat buttons for flowerpots
- 2 (⅞-inch) shank buttons for flowers
- All-purpose matching thread
- Rotary cutter, mat and ruler
- 5-inch circle template for flowers
- Basic sewing supplies and tools

INSTRUCTIONS

Project Note: *Use ¼-inch-wide seam allowances unless otherwise indicated.*

Step 1. From the large floral print, cut two 12 x 17½-inch rectangles for the tote bag front and back panels, two 10½ x 11¾-inch rectangles for the pocket and pocket lining and one 3½ x 40½-inch strip for the side/bottom panel. From the lining fabric, cut two 12 x 17½-inch rectangles and one 3½ x 41-inch strip.

Step 2. From the striped fabric, cut one 3 x 11¾-inch strip for the pocket upper-edge trim, two 3 x 10¼-inch strips for the pocket side-edge trim and two 3½ x 19-inch strips for the straps. From the coordinating geometric print for the trim and straps, cut two 4 x 10½-inch strips for the pocket side-edge trim, two 4 x 19-inch strips for the straps and two 4-inch squares for the flowerpots. From the floral scrap, cut two 5-inch circles for flowers. From the scrap of green print, cut one 4-inch square for leaves and two 1 x 4-inch strips for the stems.

Step 3. With right sides together, sew a 12 x 17½-inch bag panel to a matching lining panel. Leave a 6-inch opening on one short edge for turning. Clip the corners, turn right side out and press. Slipstitch the opening closed. Repeat with the remaining bag and lining panel. Topstitch ¼ inch from one long edge of each panel. The resulting panels should measure 11½ x 17 inches. Set aside.

Step 4. With right sides together, sew the 3½ x 40½-inch strips together, leaving a 4-inch opening in one long edge for turning. Clip the corners, turn right side out and press. Slipstitch the opening closed. Topstitch ¼ inch from each short end and set aside. Fold the strip in half crosswise and mark the fold at each finished edge with a straight pin. Set aside.

Step 5. With wrong sides together and long raw edges even, fold the 3 x 11¾-inch striped strip for the pocket trim in half. Press. With raw edges aligned, pin the folded strip to the right side at the upper edge of one pocket panel. Place the pocket lining on top with right sides together. Leaving a 4-inch opening at the lower edge for turning, stitch the lining to the pocket around all edges as shown in Fig. 1 on page 146. Clip the corners, turn right side out and press.

Step 6. Fold each remaining strip of the striped fabric and the geometric-print strips in half lengthwise with right sides together. Stitch ¼ inch from the short ends. Clip the corners, turn right side out and press. With raw edges even and upper finished edges aligned, place each piece of striped trim on top of a wider geometric-print piece. Machine-baste together ½ inch from the raw edges.

Step 7. Center the pocket on one of the prepared tote panels and use several pins to hold it in place in the center. Tuck the pieces of layered trim under the pockets with the pocket edges along the basting. Pin in place. Topstitch ¼ inch from the side and lower pocket edges as shown in Fig. 2. Remove the pins and basting.

Step 8. Locate and pin-mark the center at the bottom edge of the tote front and back panels. With centers matching and lining side to lining side, pin the side/bottom panel to the lower edge of the tote back panel. Topstitch ¼ inch from the finished edges, beginning and ending the stitching *precisely* ¼ inch from each lower corner of the back panel as shown in Fig. 3. Backstitch at the beginning and end of the seam.

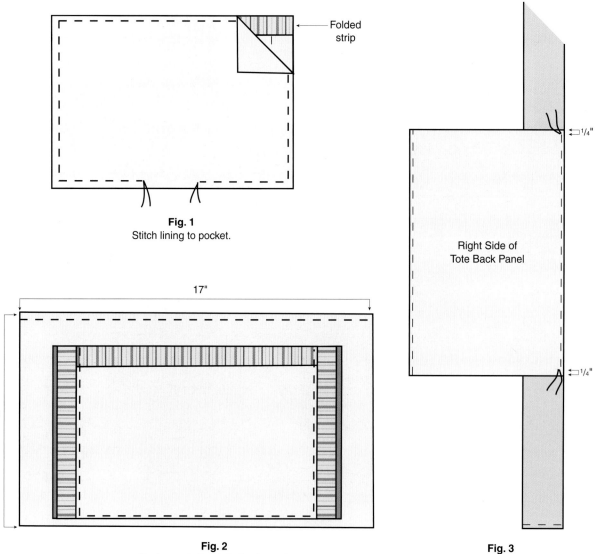

Folded strip

Fig. 1
Stitch lining to pocket.

17"

11½"

Fig. 2
Center pocket on tote front panel.
Topstitch.

Right Side of
Tote Back Panel

¼"

¼"

Fig. 3
Sew tote back to side/bottom panel.
Begin and end stitching ¼" from raw edges.

Step 9. To turn the corner, fold the side/bottom panel as shown in Fig. 4, making sure the fold that forms is at a 45-degree angle and the finished edges of the two panels are straight and even. Place a pin in the diagonal fold.

Step 10. Without disturbing the fold, turn the side/bottom panel down so the long edge is aligned with the tote panel edge. Pin in place as shown in Fig. 5. Topstitch ¼ inch from the finished edges,

beginning precisely ¼ inch from the folded edge. Repeat the folding and stitching at the opposite corner.

Step 11. Repeat Steps 8–10 to sew the tote front to the remaining finished edge of the side/bottom panel. At the bottom corners, topstitch ¼ inch from the lower folded edge as shown in Fig. 6.

Step 12. Fold each 3½ x 19-inch striped strip in half lengthwise

with right sides together and raw edges even. Stitch ¼ inch from the long edges and turn right side out. Center the seam in the back of each strip and press. Repeat with the 4 x 19-inch geometric-print straps. Center each striped strap on a geometric-print strap and pin in place. Topstitch ¼ inch from each long edge of the striped straps. Finish the short ends of each strap with closely spaced serging or zigzagging.

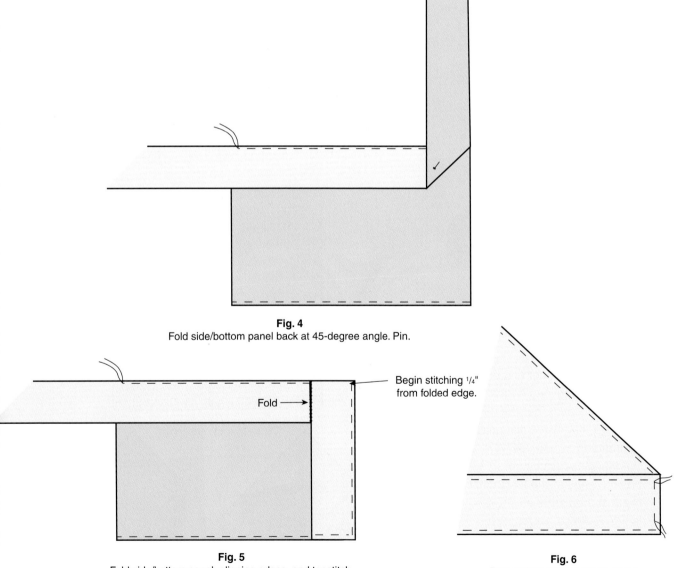

Fig. 4
Fold side/bottom panel back at 45-degree angle. Pin.

Fold ⟶

Begin stitching ¼"
from folded edge.

Fig. 5
Fold side/bottom panel, aligning edges, and topstitch.

Fig. 6
Fold and topstitch ¼" from edges
at each bottom corner.

Step 13. At the upper edge on the tote front and back, measure in and mark 1½ inches from the pocket side edges. Tuck the finished ends of the straps inside the tote where marked with at least ¾ inch of the strap end inside. Adjust the straps so they are both the same length and pin in place. Topstitch ¼ inch from the upper edge of the tote, catching the straps in the stitching. Topstitch ¼ inch below the first row of topstitching.

Step 14. For flowers, machine baste ¼ inch from the raw edge of each circle. With the circles face down, pull the bobbin threads to gather the circles into yo-yo flowers as shown in Fig. 7. Flatten the circles and sew a ¾-inch shank button in the center of the gathered opening of each flower.

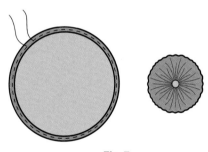

Fig. 7
Draw up bobbin threads to make yo-yos.

Step 15. Turn under and press ¼ inch on both long edges of each stem. For leaves, cut the 4-inch square in half twice diagonally to create four triangles. With the triangles face down, fold the pointed ends of the long side in to meet in the center as shown in Fig. 8. Press.

Step 16. With each flowerpot square face down, draw fold lines

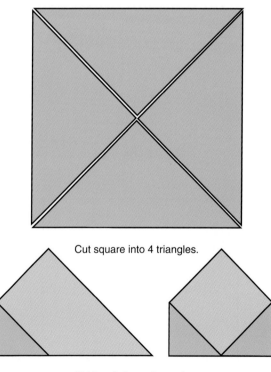

Cut square into 4 triangles.

Fold ends to center and press.

Fig. 8

as shown in Fig. 9. Turn under and press along the lines. At the upper and lower edges, turn under and press ⅜ inch. On the right side of each flowerpot, stitch or glue a piece of satin ribbon ½ inch below the upper edge. Sew a ½-inch flat button in the center of the ribbon on each flowerpot.

Step 17. Referring to the photo for placement, position the flowers, leaves, stems and flowerpots on the tote bag. With the leaves tucked under the stems and the stems tucked under the flowers and flowerpots, glue or edgestitch the pieces in place. ∎

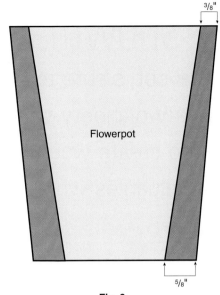

Fig. 9
Mark edges, turn and press.

Cheery Snowman Scarf & Hat Set

This whimsical set is sure to keep you toasty warm on blustery days. Two cheery snowmen at the scarf ends are open in back to create warm pockets for your hands—or a place to tuck valuables while you're out for a winter stroll.

DESIGNS BY DEBRA QUARTERMAIN

PROJECT SPECIFICATIONS
Skill Level: Beginner
Scarf Size: 8 x 35½ inches
Hat Size: 24 inches around brim, 11 inches tall

MATERIALS
- 15 x 60-inch strip of blue (snowflake) fleece
- ⅓ yard white fleece
- 3 (½-inch) blue buttons
- 2 (¼-inch) black buttons
- 4 (½-inch) black buttons
- Polyester fiberfill
- Permanent fabric adhesive
- Red embroidery floss
- All-purpose matching thread
- Powder blush
- Embroidery and hand-sewing needles
- Ruler
- Air-soluble marking pen
- 7-inch circle template
- Basic sewing supplies and tools

INSTRUCTIONS
Scarf

Project Note: *Measurements given will fit a teen to adult-size head (24-inch circumference). Adjust the hat dimensions as needed to fit the individual.*

Step 1. From the blue fleece, cut one 9 x 57-inch strip for the scarf, two 4 x 24-inch strips for the hat brim, one 3 x 10-inch rectangle for the snowman's scarf on the hat, two ¾ x 1-inch rectangles for snowman noses on the scarf and one ⅜ x ½-inch rectangle for the nose on the hat. From the white fleece, cut one 12 x 24-inch strip for the hat and four 7-inch circles for the scarf snowmen.

Step 2. Referring to Fig. 1, draw a line across one white circle using the air-soluble marking pen. Cut along the line. Repeat with the remaining circles to make 4 identical snowman heads.

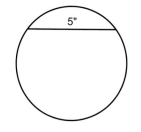

Fig. 1
Draw a 5"-long line on the circle.
Cut on the line.

Step 3. Referring to Fig. 2 and using the air-soluble marking pen,

draw positioning marks for the facial features on each of two white snowman heads. Sew ½-inch black buttons for eyes in place. Use 3 strands of red embroidery floss and a running stitch to make the mouths. Trim away the corners of the two ⅜ x ½-inch blue rectangles to form ovals for the noses. Glue or stitch a nose to each head.

Fig. 2
Mark and sew facial features in place
on white faces.

Step 4. Turn under and press ½ inch along the straight edge of each of the two remaining snowman heads. Stitch or glue in place. The fleece will not ravel so there is no need to finish the raw edge.

Step 5. With right sides together, pin each snowman head to one of the remaining white pieces. Stitch ¼ inch from the round edges, leaving the straight edges open

for turning as shown in Fig. 3. Turn right side out.

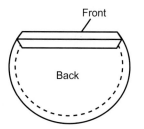

Fig. 3
Sew front and back heads together.
Make two.

Step 6. Center a snowman head at one short end of the scarf panel on the right side and pin in place. Stitch ¼ inch from the raw edges as shown in Fig. 4, keeping the back of the head free of the stitching to create a pocket at each end of the scarf. Repeat with the remaining head at the opposite end of the scarf.

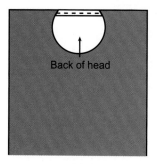

Fig. 4
Center and stitch head to scarf end.

Step 7. Trim the scarf at each edge of the snowman heads as shown in Fig. 5.

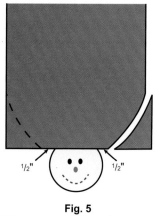

Fig. 5
Trim and round off scarf corners.

Step 8. Turn under and press ½ inch at each long edge of the scarf. Topstitch ³/₈-inch from the turned edges.

INSTRUCTIONS
Hat
Step 1. With right sides facing, stitch the brim pieces together ¼ inch from one long edge. Finger press the seam open. With right sides together and seam lines matching, stitch the short ends of the brim together. Press the seam open. Turn the brim right side out and fold with raw edges even.

Step 2. Fold the white rectangle for the hat in half with right sides together and stitch ¼ inch from the long raw edges to form the center back seam. Press the seam open.

Step 3. With seam lines matching in back and all raw edges even, pin the brim to the right side of one edge of the hat. Stitch ¼ inch from the raw edges and turn the brim down so the seam allowance is inside the hat. Hand- or machine-baste ¼ inch from hat upper raw edge and leave thread tails (Fig 6).

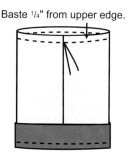

Baste ¼" from upper edge.

Fig. 6
Sew brim to lower edge of hat.

Step 4. Turn the hat wrong side out. Pull the stitches tight on the wrong side of the hat to close the

opening and secure the threads by tying in a knot or taking several stitches through the layers with a hand-sewing needle. Turn the hat right side out.

Step 5. At each end of the strip for the snowman's scarf, make 1-inch-long slashes spaced ⅛ inch apart for the fringe.

Step 6. With the hat right side out, tuck a ball of fiberfill into the gathered top and tie the snowman's scarf under it to create the snowman's head.

Step 7. Referring to the photo, mark the placement for eyes, nose and mouth on the snowman head. To attach ¼-inch buttons in place for the eyes, begin by anchoring the thread in the neck underneath the scarf at the back seam of the hat. Bring the needle to the right side of the head and sew buttons in place. Use three strands of red embroidery floss to do a running stitch for the mouth. Trim the corners away on the ⅜ x ½-inch rectangle to make an oval

for the nose. Stitch or glue nose in place. For cheeks, gently brush on a bit of powdered blush.

Step 8. To form the brim, turn up 2¾ inches at the lower edge. Tack in place by hand or machine stitching through all layers of fabric at the center back seam. Using a few hand stitches, catch only the brim inner layer to the hat in front. Evenly space and sew three blue buttons down the front of the hat. ■

Yummy Snowman Aprons

It's so easy to whip up matching aprons for a special mom and her child. Our sassy snowmen aprons are sure to be a big help in the kitchen making cookies for the holidays.

DESIGN BY ANGIE WILHITE

PROJECT SPECIFICATIONS
Skill Level: Beginner
Size: Adult and Child

MATERIALS
Materials listed are for an adult-size and child-size apron.

- 1 yard 44/45-inch-wide white linen or firm cotton fabric; do not choose a poly blend
- Scraps of white, black and orange cotton fabric (facial features)
- All-purpose thread to match fabrics
- Rayon embroidery thread (black and orange)
- ¼ yard paper-backed fusible web
- ¼ yard tear-away stabilizer
- Temporary spray adhesive
- Liquid seam sealant or permanent fabric glue
- 5½ yards ⅞-inch-wide white grosgrain ribbon for neck loops and ties
- Pencil
- Water- or air-soluble marking pen
- 14 (⅝-inch-diameter) black buttons
- Rotary cutter, mat and ruler
- Basic sewing supplies and tools

INSTRUCTIONS
Step 1. Prewash the fabric; do not use fabric softener. Press to remove wrinkles.

Step 2. For the adult apron, cut a 20 x 31-inch rectangle from the white fabric. For the child's apron, cut a 14 x 22-inch rectangle.

Step 3. Referring to Fig. 1, cut away a triangle at the upper edge of each apron panel to create the armhole edges for the casing.

Step 4. Turn under and press ³/₈ inch on each long edge of each apron. Turn under again and press to make a double hem. Edgestitch. Hem the lower edge of each rectangle in the same manner.

Step 5. Turn under and press ¼ inch at each armhole edge. Turn under 1¼ inches and press to create the armhole casing. Edgestitch each casing in place as shown in Fig. 2 on page 156.

Step 6. To make patterns for adult-size apron, draw a 2¼-inch circle for the eye, a 1⅞-inch circle for the pupil and a 2 x 6 x 6-inch triangle for the nose. For child-size apron, you will need the 1⅞-inch circle for the eye, a 1½-inch circle for the pupil and a 1⅜ x 4½ x 4½-inch triangle for the nose.

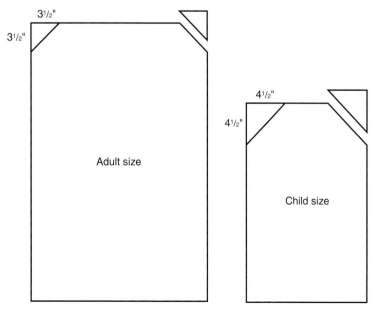

Fig. 1
Cut away upper corners.

Step 7. Trace the patterns for the pupils, eyes and nose on the paper side of the fusible web, leaving ½ inch of space between the shapes. Cut out each shape leaving a ¼-inch-wide margin beyond the drawn lines.

Step 8. Following the manufacturer's directions, apply the pieces to the wrong side of the appropriate fabrics—white for the eyes, black for the pupils and orange for the nose. Cut out the shapes on the drawn lines.

Step 9. Referring to Fig. 3, position the eyes and nose on the apron fronts and fuse in place following manufacturer's directions. On each apron, mark the button positions for seven buttons for the mouth, spacing them approximately 1 inch apart.

Step 10. Using a light coat of temporary spray adhesive, apply the tear-away stabilizer to the wrong side of each apron underneath the facial-feature appliqués.

Step 11. Using rayon embroidery thread in the top of the machine and matching all-purpose thread in the bobbin, satin-stitch around each appliqué. Pull top threads to the underside and tie off securely, then dab with seam sealant or permanent fabric glue for added security. Test-stitch first on a sample and adjust tensions and stitch width and length as needed for

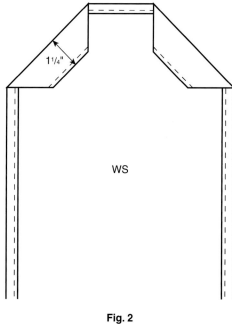

Fig. 2
Make 1¼"-wide hems at armhole edges for casings.

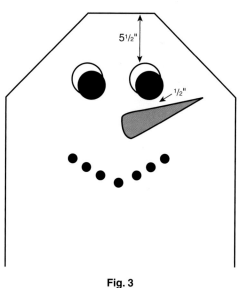

Fig. 3
Position and fuse eyes, pupils and nose in place.

smooth coverage. To satin-stitch the nose, begin at the point and end at the point, overlapping the first stitches. Gently tear away the stabilizer on the underside of each apron.

Step 12. Sew buttons in place for the mouth on each apron.

Step 13. Cut the grosgrain ribbon into two lengths, one 3 yards long and one 2½ yards long. Cut the

ends at 45-degree angles. Thread the longer piece through the armhole casings of the adult apron. Repeat with the shorter length for the child's apron. ■

Fun Pocket Bibs

Make these cheerful bibs for a special baby shower gift. They are quick and easy to make so you can sew several in an afternoon.

DESIGNS BY CAROL DACE

PROJECT SPECIFICATIONS
Skill Level: Beginner
Bib Size: Approximately 11 x 12½ inches

MATERIALS

HEART BIB
- 1 white terrycloth fingertip towel
- 1 yard pink extra-wide, double-fold bias tape
- 3½-inch square prewashed pink print
- Scrap of fusible web
- 5-inch square of tear-away stabilizer
- Pink all-purpose thread
- Air- or water-soluble marking pen
- 6-inch paper circle
- Basic sewing supplies and tools

INSTRUCTIONS
Heart Bib
Project Note: Fingertip towels are approximately 11 x 18 inches, including the fringe.

Step 1. For the neckline template, fold the 6-inch paper circle in half and crease. Fold in half again and crease to mark the center.

Step 2. Remove the tag from the towel and place the towel face up on a flat surface. Turn down the upper edge, folding it 1 inch from the point where the fringe begins as shown in Fig. 1. Pin in place and topstitch ½ inch from the fold. Repeat at the lower edge, but turn under to the wrong side of the towel. Fold the towel in half lengthwise and mark for the neckline center. Unfold and center the neckline template with the long edge along the upper folded edge. Use an air- or water-soluble marking pen to trace around the half-circle. Cut on the line.

Step 3. Cut a 34-inch-long piece of bias tape, fold in half and mark the center. Fold the bib in half lengthwise and mark the neckline center. Matching the center marks, encase the neckline edge in the bias tape and pin in place. Make sure the widest fold of the bias tape is on the underside. Beginning at one end of the bias tape, edgestitch the layers together, continuing around the neckline and the remaining end of the tape as shown in Fig. 2 on page 160.

Step 4. Turn the bottom edge up onto the bib right side (see photo) to make a 2½-inch-wide pocket. Stitch ¼ inch from the short ends.

Step 5. Draw a heart shape onto the paper side of the fusible web. Following the manufacturer's

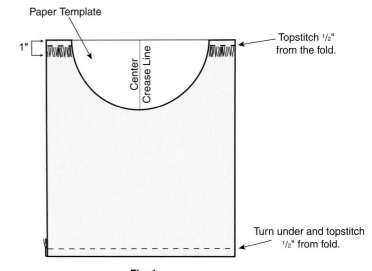

Paper Template

1"

Center Crease Line

Topstitch ½" from the fold.

Turn under and topstitch ½" from fold.

Fig. 1
Trace around template and cut along traced lines.

directions, apply fusible web to the wrong side of the pink print for the heart. Cut out and remove the backing paper. Position on the bib (see photo) and fuse in place.

Step 6. Pin the tear-away stabilizer underneath the heart on the bib wrong side. Set the machine for a close, medium-width satin stitch. Beginning and ending at the point,

satin-stitch over the raw edges of the heart. Pull the threads to the underside and tie off. Remove the stabilizer.

MATERIALS

BALLOON BIB

- 1 off-white terrycloth fingertip towel
- 1 yard red extra-wide, double-fold bias tape
- 2½-inch squares prewashed red, blue and yellow solid-color cotton fabrics
- Scraps of fusible web
- 4 x 7-inch piece of tear-away stabilizer
- Red, blue and yellow all-purpose threads
- Air- or water-soluble marking pen
- Basic sewing supplies and tools

INSTRUCTIONS
Balloon Bib

Step 1. Follow Steps 1–4 for the Heart Bib, using red thread to topstitch the folds.

Step 2. Draw three balloons onto the paper side of the fusible web leaving ½ inch between the shapes. Cut out each balloon, leaving a paper margin around each one. Following the manufacturer's directions, apply a balloon shape to each piece of solid-colored fabric (red, yellow, blue). Cut out each balloon and remove the backing paper. Referring to the photo, position the balloons on the bib and fuse in place. Use the air- or water-soluble pen to draw balloon strings as shown in the photo.

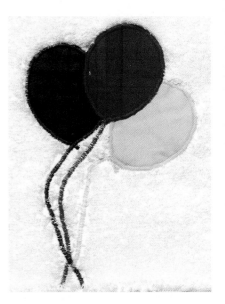

Step 3. Thread the machine with blue thread and topstitch ⅛ inch above the red topstitching on the pocket. Adjust the machine for a closely spaced, narrow satin stitch and stitch over the raw edges of the blue balloon, beginning and ending at the edges of the red balloon. Satin stitch the string.

Step 4. Change to yellow thread and satin-stitch the yellow balloon and string. Change to a straight stitch and add a row of yellow topstitching between the rows of blue and red topstitching. Change to red thread and satin-stitch the red balloon and string. Leave the red thread on the machine.

Step 5. Turn the bottom edge up onto the bib right side (see photo on page 159) to make a 2½-inch-wide pocket. Stitch ¼ inch from the short ends. ∎

Fig. 2
Encase neckline in bias tape.

Fun Floral Jacket

Felt appliqués and hand embroidery turn a simple little wool jacket into a delightful flower garden for a favorite baby.

DESIGN BY JUNE FIECHTER

INSTRUCTIONS
Step 1. From the jacket fabric, cut one piece 15½ x 23 inches for the jacket body and two 11-inch squares for the sleeves. Referring to Fig. 1 on page 162, slash the jacket body strip to create an opening and cut out the circle for the neckline. Fold the panel in half

crosswise and make a ⅛-inch-long clip at each inner and outer raw edge to mark the shoulders. Fold in half lengthwise and make a snip at the neckline center back.

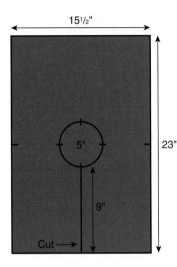

Fig. 1
Cut the front edge and neckline opening.

Step 2. Referring to Fig. 2, reshape the front edges of the neckline.

Fig. 2
Cut away corners to reshape the front neckline.

Step 3. With the wrong side of the jacket panel facing you, measure 2½ inches from the neck edge at the clip and mark. Using a chalk pencil, draw a double-pointed dart

that is 1 inch wide at the shoulder mark and tapers to nothing 5 inches below the shoulder at each end as shown in Fig. 3. Draw a ½ x 4-inch dart at the center of the back neckline.

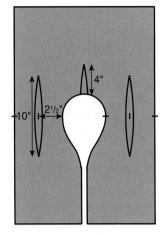

Fig. 3
Draw dart stitching lines.

Step 4. Stitch the darts and slash along the fold to within ½ inch of the points. Press the darts open as shown in Fig. 4.

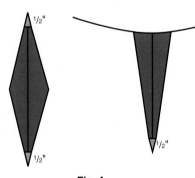

Fig. 4
Slash darts along the fold line and press open.

Step 5. Trim each sleeve panel as shown in Fig. 5. Snip the center.

Step 6. With right sides together and the center snip of the sleeve matching the shoulder snip, pin the sleeves to the jacket panel and stitch ⅜ inch from the raw edges,

Fig. 5
Reshape the upper edge of each sleeve.

ending the stitching ⅜ inch from the underarm raw edges of the sleeve as shown in Fig. 6. Press the seam open.

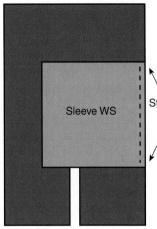

Fig. 6
Sew sleeves to jacket body.

Step 7. Complete the sleeve underarm seam and press open. Stitch the jacket side seams and press open. If desired, topstitch ¼ inch from the seam line on each side of each seam.

Step 8. Turn under and press ½ inch at the lower edge of the jacket. Topstitch ¼ inch from the pressed edge.

Step 9. From green wool felt, cut one 2-inch-diameter circle. From the blue wool felt, cut one ¾-inch-diameter and one 1¼-inch-diameter circle. From the pink wool felt, cut one ¾-inch-diameter circle.

Step 10. Referring to Fig. 7, arrange the felt circles on the jacket front and pin in place. Do a running stitch with yarn to anchor the circles with petal shapes.

Step 11. Using wool yarn, blanket-stitch over the raw edges of the front opening and back neckline as shown in Fig. 8. Space the stitches ⅜ inch apart and make them ⅜ inch deep.

Step 12. Sew buttons in place on the right front, spacing them evenly. Glue hook-and-loop dot closures in place under the buttons.

Step 13. Roll the cuffs up twice from the bottom edge to create sleeves of the correct length for the baby. ∎

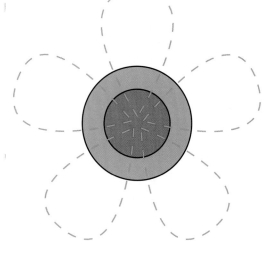

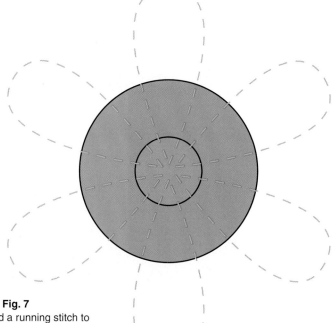

Fig. 7
Use yarn and a running stitch to
make flower petals and secure the circles.

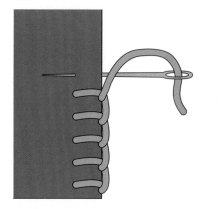

Fig. 8
Blanket-stitch over the raw edges.

Simply Summer

Rickrack trim edges the contrast band and pockets on this sweet summer dress. It all adds up to fun in the sun for a favorite child.

DESIGN BY JUDITH SANDSTROM

PROJECT SPECIFICATIONS

Skill Level: Confident beginner

Sundress Size: Size 4 and 5, with yardage and cutting dimensions for size 2 and 3 in parentheses

MATERIALS

Note: Choose 44/45-inch-wide cotton for this dress.

- ⅝ (½) yard summery print for the dress
- ¼ (¼) yard contrasting solid for the bodice band and straps
- 1 package ½-inch-wide rickrack trim
- All-purpose thread to match fabric
- Rotary cutter, mat and ruler
- Basic sewing supplies and tools

INSTRUCTIONS

Project Note: Use ¼-inch-wide seam allowances unless otherwise noted and stitch all seams with right sides together.

Step 1. From the print for the dress, cut two 22-inch (17-inch) squares. From the solid, cut the following pieces: four 3 x 10-inch (2½ x 7½-inch) pieces for the front and back upper bands and band facings; four 2½ x 9-inch (2½ x 6-inch) strips for the straps; and two 3½ x 4-inch (3 x 3½-inch) pieces for the pockets.

Step 2. At the side and bottom edges of each pocket, turn under and press ¼ inch. Turn under and press ¼ inch along the upper edge. Turn again and topstitch in place.

Step 3. Allowing extra rickrack at the upper edge of the pocket, position the trim under the pressed side and bottom edges of each pocket so only half the width shows. Turn under the raw ends

so they are even with the pocket upper edge. Edgestitch in place.

Step 4. Position and pin each pocket to one of the 22-inch (17-inch) squares. Place 9½ inches above the bottom edge and 4 inches in from the side edges. Stitch in place, backstitching at the upper edges for added security. Machine-baste ½ inch from the upper side edges as shown in Fig. 1.

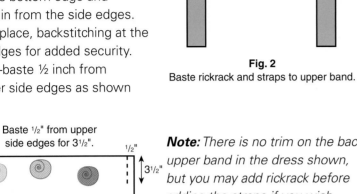

Fig. 2
Baste rickrack and straps to upper band.

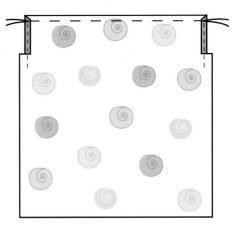

Fig. 3
Clip 3" from upper edge.
Make narrow double hems.
Machine-baste ¼" from upper edge.

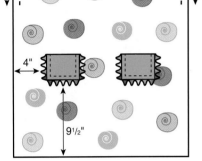

Fig. 1
Stitch pockets in place.

Baste ½" from upper side edges for 3½".
1/2" 1/2" 3½" 3½" 4" 9½"

Step 5. With right sides together, fold each strap in half lengthwise and stitch ¼ inch from the long edges and one short edge. Clip the corners. Turn right side out and press.

Step 6. Cut one 10-inch-long (7½-inch-long) piece of rickrack. Position on the right side of a band with the points even with the raw edge as shown in Fig. 2. Machine-baste in place. Position the straps on the rickrack-trimmed band and baste in place, again referring to Fig. 2. Baste the remaining straps to the upper edge of one of the remaining bands for the back.

Note: There is no trim on the back upper band in the dress shown, but you may add rickrack before adding the straps if you wish.

Step 7. Clip to the basting on each side of the dress front and back, 3 inches from the upper edge. Turn under and press double, narrrow hems along the 3 inches; edgestitch.

Step 8. Machine-baste ¼ inch from the upper raw edge of each square as shown in Fig. 3. With right sides together and the square facing you, pin the square with pockets to the rickrack-trimmed band. Place the hemmed edges of the square ¼ inch in from the short ends of the band. Pull on the bobbin threads to gather the square to fit. Pin and stitch. Press the seam toward the band as shown in Fig. 4. Repeat with the remaining square and band with straps for the back.

Step 9. Turn under and press ¼ inch along one long edge of each upper band facing. With right sides together and raw edges aligned, stitch a facing to the

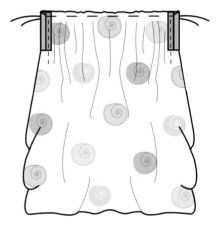

Fig. 4
Draw up gathers and stitch dress to band.

upper edge of the front and back band along the side and upper edges as shown in Fig. 5 on page 169. Clip the corners. Turn right side out and press. Pin the facing in place along the stitching line and slipstitch in place.

Step 10. Using ½-inch-wide seams, sew the front and back together at the sides. Serge or zigzag-finish the seam edges together and press the seam allowances toward the back.

Step 11. Serge-finish the lower edge of the dress (or turn under and press ¼ inch), then turn an additional 1½-inch hem allowance. Edgestitch the fold in place or slipstitch by hand. ■

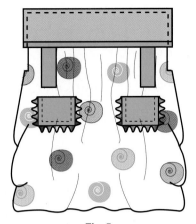

Fig. 5
Stitch facing to upper band.

Reversible Rainbow Baby Blanket

Cut and flatlock-serge colorful flannel squares together to create this warm blanket for a favorite baby.

DESIGN BY NANCY FIEDLER

PROJECT SPECIFICATIONS
Skill Level: Beginner
Blanket Size: 48 x 60 inches

MATERIALS

- ¾ yard each of 8 bright flannel prints
- 5 spools rayon thread
- 1 cone (3,000 yards) variegated quilting thread
- Temporary spray adhesive
- Rotary-cutting tools
- Serger
- Basic sewing supplies and tools

INSTRUCTIONS
Step 1. Cut two strips 4¼ x 27 inches on the lengthwise grain from each of the eight flannels. Cut each strip into 4¼-inch squares.

Step 2. Cut four squares each 12½ x 12½ inches from the eight flannels.

Step 3. Set up the serger for a two-thread flatlock stitch, placing the quilting thread in the needle and the rayon thread in the lower looper. For sergers that do not have a two-thread function, set up the machine for a three-thread flatlock. Place the rayon thread in the upper looper, the quilting thread in the needle and all-purpose serger thread in the lower looper.

Step 4. Select two coordinating colors from the 4¼-inch squares. Place two squares wrong sides together and serge without cutting off any fabric. Gently pull the squares apart to form the flatlock seam. Add a third square as shown in Fig. 1 to form the first strip of a Nine-Patch block. Follow Fig. 1 to make three more strips. Sew the three strips together to make a Nine-Patch block. Make a total of eight Nine-Patch blocks in any combination of colors for a scrappy effect.

Step 5. On a flat work surface, arrange the blocks as desired in five rows of four blocks each. Label blocks as shown in Fig. 2.

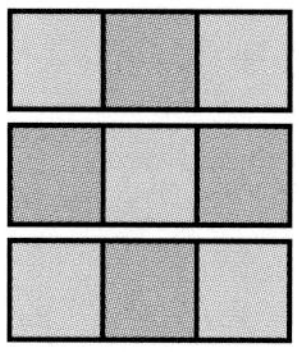

Fig. 1
Make Nine-Patch block as shown.

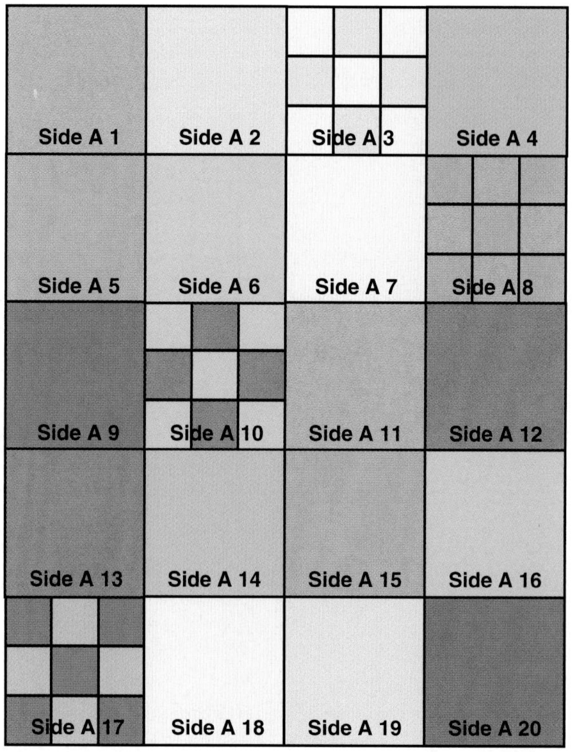

Side A 1	Side A 2	Side A 3	Side A 4
Side A 5	Side A 6	Side A 7	Side A 8
Side A 9	Side A 10	Side A 11	Side A 12
Side A 13	Side A 14	Side A 15	Side A 16
Side A 17	Side A 18	Side A 19	Side A 20

Fig. 2
Arrange as desired; label blocks as shown.

Step 6. With remaining blocks, repeat arrangement and label blocks Side B 1, Side B 2, etc.

Step 7. Spray the wrong side of each block with temporary adhesive. Place each numbered A block wrong side to wrong side on the corresponding numbered block of Side B. Carefully smooth the blocks together, keeping edges even.

Step 8. Measure and square all blocks to 12¼ x 12¼ inches.

Step 9. Flatlock each row of blocks together.

Step 10. Serge the rows together, opening each flatlock seam.

Step 12. Set up serger for a two-thread wrapped overcast stitch and serge over the raw edges to finish the blanket. ■

Metric Conversion Charts

Metric Conversions

U.S. Measurement		Multiplied by		Metric Measurement
yards	x	.9144	=	meters (m)
yards	x	91.44	=	centimeters (cm)
inches	x	2.54	=	centimeters (cm)
inches	x	25.40	=	millimeters (mm)
inches	x	.0254	=	meters (m)

Metric Measurement		Multiplied by		U.S. Measurement
centimeters	x	.3937	=	inches
meters	x	1.0936	=	yards

Standard Equivalents

U.S. Measurement		Metric Measurement		
1/8 inch	=	3.20 mm	=	0.32 cm
1/4 inch	=	6.35 mm	=	0.635 cm
3/8 inch	=	9.50 mm	=	0.95 cm
1/2 inch	=	12.70 mm	=	1.27 cm
5/8 inch	=	15.90 mm	=	1.59 cm
3/4 inch	=	19.10 mm	=	1.91 cm
7/8 inch	=	22.20 mm	=	2.22 cm
1 inch	=	25.40 mm	=	2.54 cm
1/8 yard	=	11.43 cm	=	0.11 m
1/4 yard	=	22.86 cm	=	0.23 m
3/8 yard	=	34.29 cm	=	0.34 m
1/2 yard	=	45.72 cm	=	0.46 m
5/8 yard	=	57.15 cm	=	0.57 m
3/4 yard	=	68.58 cm	=	0.69 m
7/8 yard	=	80.00 cm	=	0.80 m
1 yard	=	91.44 cm	=	0.91 m

U.S. Measurement		Metric Measurement		
1 1/8 yard	=	102.87 cm	=	1.03 m
1 1/4 yard	=	114.30 cm	=	1.14 m
1 3/8 yard	=	125.73 cm	=	1.26 m
1 1/2 yard	=	137.16 cm	=	1.37 m
1 5/8 yard	=	148.59 cm	=	1.49 m
1 3/4 yard	=	160.02 cm	=	1.60 m
1 7/8 yard	=	171.44 cm	=	1.71 m
2 yards	=	182.88 cm	=	1.83 m
2 1/8 yards	=	194.31 cm	=	1.94 m
2 1/4 yards	=	205.74 cm	=	2.06 m
2 3/8 yards	=	217.17 cm	=	2.17 m
2 1/2 yards	=	228.60 cm	=	2.29 m
2 5/8 yards	=	240.03 cm	=	2.40 m
2 3/4 yards	=	251.46 cm	=	2.51 m
2 7/8 yards	=	262.88 cm	=	2.63 m
3 yards	=	274.32 cm	=	2.74 m
3 1/8 yards	=	285.75 cm	=	2.86 m
3 1/4 yards	=	297.18 cm	=	2.97 m
3 3/8 yards	=	308.61 cm	=	3.09 m
3 1/2 yards	=	320.04 cm	=	3.20 m
3 5/8 yards	=	331.47 cm	=	3.31 m
3 3/4 yards	=	342.90 cm	=	3.43 m
3 7/8 yards	=	354.32 cm	=	3.54 m
4 yards	=	365.76 cm	=	3.66 m
4 1/8 yards	=	377.19 cm	=	3.77 m
4 1/4 yards	=	388.62 cm	=	3.89 m
4 3/8 yards	=	400.05 cm	=	4.00 m
4 1/2 yards	=	411.48 cm	=	4.11 m
4 5/8 yards	=	422.91 cm	=	4.23 m
4 3/4 yards	=	434.34 cm	=	4.34 m
4 7/8 yards	=	445.76 cm	=	4.46 m
5 yards	=	457.20 cm	=	4.57 m

Fabrics & Supplies

Page 10: *Rainbow Sailboats Ensemble*—Thin cotton batting from Hobbs Bonded Fibers and Wonder Under from Pellon Consumer Products and Wonder Under from Pellon Consumer Products.

Page 19: *Pacific Isle Bedroom Ensemble*—Jumbo welting from Hollywood Trims division of Dritz/Prym-Dritz Corp., Steam-A-Seam 2 fusible adhesive tape from Warm & Natural/The Warm Company, Wailea Coast #667710 for duvet reverse side, #667730 Tikki fabric for dust ruffle and sham borders and #648725 Tobago fabric for welting from Waverly Fabric.

Page 30: *Diamond Suede Quilt*—Velvet pigskin suede from The Leather Factory and Quilter's Choice Basting Glue from Beacon Adhesives.

Page 45: *Tulip Tablecloth*—Wonder-Under from Pellon Consumer Products and rotary-cutting tools from Fiskars Inc.

Page 48: *Reversible Table Runners*—Fabri-Tac permanent fabric adhesive from Beacon Adhesives and Wonder Tape double-sided, self-adhesive basting tape from Dritz/Prym-Dritz Corp.

Page 53: *Custom-Fit Table & Chair Covers*—Covered button forms from Dritz/Prym-Dritz Corp., sheer ribbons from Mokuba Ribbons Co. and Camelia Terrace #667593 floral print Wynfield Manor #649016 all over print fabrics from Waverly Fabrics.

Page 81: *Roly-Poly Snowman Dolls*—Sculpey oven-bake clay, sweet potato 033 from Polyform Products Co./Sculpey.

Page 85: *Autumn Floral Duo*—Cotton batting from Warm & Natural/The Warm Company.

Page 87: *Beach Cover-Up & Matching Tote*—Wonder-Under, Craft Bond and Stitch-n-Tear from Pellon Consumer Products.

Page 97: *Side-Slit Skirt & Scarf*—Scarf fringe from Hollywood Trims division of Dritz/Prym-Dritz Corp. and Steam-A-Seam 2 fusible adhesive tape from Warm & Natural/The Warm Company.

Page 105: *Sophisticate in Plaid*—Craft-Bond from Pellon Consumer Products.

Page 121: *Snuggle Sack*—Wonder Tape double-sided, self-adhesive basting tape from Dritz/Prym-Dritz Corp. and decorative snaps from Snap Source.

Page 124: *Suede-Trimmed Wool Jacket*—Fabri-Tac permanent fabric adhesive from Beacon Adhesives, Wonder Tape self-adhesive, double-sided basting tape from Dritz/Prym-Dritz Corp. and suede from The Leather Factory.

Page 133: *Lined Denim Tote*—Aleene's Stop Fraying and Aleene's Jewel-It Embellishing Glue from Duncan Enterprises and #8 fine braid #011HL gun metal from Kreinik Mfg. Co. Inc.

Page 136: *Tote Bag Trio*—Steam-A-Seam 2 fusible adhesive tape from Warm & Natural/The Warm Company and Fabri-Quilt quilted fabrics and border fabrics from Jackman's Fabrics.

Page 144: *Spring Garden Tote Bag*—Fabri-Tac permanent fabric adhesive from Beacon Adhesives.

Page 150: *Cheery Snowman Scarf & Hat Set*—Fabri-Tac permanent fabric adhesive from Beacon Adhesives.

Page 155: *Yummy Snowman Aprons*—Wonder-Under and Stitch-n-Tear from Pellon Consumer Products, Dual Duty Plus all-purpose and rayon embroidery threads from Coats & Clark/J. & P. Coats and Peoria black buttons from JHB International Inc.

Page 161: *Fun Floral Jacket*— #95237097 3-piece Rotary-Cutting Center and #98827797 Softgrip No. 8 Bent scissors from Fiskars Inc., #90008 white fasteners from Velcro USA Inc. and Aleene's Jewel-It Embellishing Glue from Duncan Enterprises.

Page 165: *Simply Summer Sundress*—Rainbow rickrack from Wrights.

Page 170: *Reversible Rainbow Baby Blanket*—YLI Pearl Crown rayon thread and YLI Colours variegated quilting thread.

Contact Information

The following companies provided fabric and/or supplies for projects in *Pattern-free Sewing*. If you are unable to locate a product locally, contact the manufacturers listed below for the closest retail or mail-order source in your area.

Beacon Adhesives
(800) 865-7238
www.beacon1.com

Coats & Clark/J. & P. Coats
(800) 648-1479
www.coatsandclark.com

Dritz/Prym-Dritz Corp.
www.dritz.com

Duncan Enterprises
(800) 438-6226
www.duncan-enterprises.com

Fiskars Inc.
(800) 950-0203
www.fiskars.com

Hobbs Bonded Fibers
www.hobbsbondedfibers.com

Jackman's Fabrics
(800) 758-3742
www.jackmansfabrics.com

JHB International Inc.
(303) 751-8100
www.buttons.com

Kreinik Mfg. Co. Inc.
(800) 537-2166
www.kreinik.com

Mokuba Ribbon Company
www.jkmribbon.com

Pellon Consumer Products
(919) 620-7457
www.pellonideas.com

Polyform Products Co./ Sculpey
www.sculpey.com

Snap Source
(800) 725-4600
www.snapsource.com

Tandy Leather Factory
(800) 433-3201
www.tandyleather.com

The Leather Co.
(713) 880-8235
www.leatherfactory.com

Velcro USA Inc.
www.Velcro.com

Warm & Natural/The Warm Company
(800) 234-9276
www.warmcompany.com

Wayerly Fabrics
www.waverly.com

Wrights
(413) 436-7732

YLI Corporation
(800) 296-8139
www.ylicorp.com

Special Thanks

We would like to thank the talented sewing designers whose work is featured in this collection.

Mary Ayres
Autumn Floral Duo, 85

Lori Blankenship
Beach Cover Up & Matching Tote, 87
Beaded Chenille Poncho, 115
Sophisticate in Plaid, 105

Patricia Converse
Diamond Suede Quilt, 30

Carol Dace
Fun Pocket Bibs, 158
Handy Bag Holder, 74

June Fiechter
Fun Floral Jacket, 161
Lined Denim Tote, 133

Nancy Fiedler
Fleecy Fringed Poncho, 118
Reversible Rainbow Baby Blanket, 170

Pearl Louise Krush
Checkerboard Kitchen Collection, 67
Sassy Classy Lady, 99
Vintage Charm Pillows, 35

Lee Lindeman
Decorative Fabric Trees, 77
Roly-Poly Snowman Dolls, 81

Chris Malone
Cheery Yo-Yos Table Set, 61

Sheri McCrimmon
Snowmen Bearing Gifts, 79

Debra Quartermain
Cheery Snowman Scarf & Hat Set, 150
Spring Garden Tote Bag, 144

Judith Sandstrom
Rainbow Sailboats Ensemble, 10
Simply Summer, 165
Tulip Tablecloth, 45

Carla Schwab
Casual Drawstring Shoulder Bag, 141

Marian Shenk
All-Occasion Sweatshirt Jacket, 128
Crazy-Patch Throw, 28
Tasseled Valance Panels, 58

Julie Weaver
Crazy Block Chenille Throw, 7
It's a Wrap, 43
Pleasant Dreams, 16
Simply Floral, Simply Round, 38

Angie Wilhite
Yummy Snowman Aprons, 155

Carol Zentgraf
Checkerboard Wrap Skirt, 113
Custom-Fit Table & Chair Covers, 53
Free-as-a Breeze Sundress, 93
Pacific Isle Bedroom Ensemble, 19
Reversible Table Runners, 48
Side-Slit Skirt & Scarf, 97
Snuggle Sack, 121
Suede-Trimmed Wool Jacket, 124
Tote Bag Trio, 136